PENGUIN BOOKS

BOYS AND GIRLS FOREVER

Alison Lurie is the author of many highly praised novels, including *The War Between the Tates, The Truth About Lorin Jones, Foreign Affairs,* and *The Last Resort.* She has also written a book on the meaning of fashion, *The Language of Clothes,* and a collection of essays on children's literature, *Don't Tell the Grown-Ups.* Her most recent book is *Familiar Spirits: A Memoir of James Merrill and David Jackson.* She teaches writing, folklore, and literature at Cornell University.

BOYS AND GIRLS & FOREVER

Children's Classics from Cinderella to Harry Potter

Alison Lurie

PENGUIN BOOKS

PENGUIN BOOKS

Published by the Penguin Group

Penguin Putnam Inc., 375 Hudson Street, New York, New York 10014, U.S.A.
Penguin Books Ltd, 80 Strand, London WC2R 0RL, England
Penguin Books Australia Ltd, 250 Camberwell Road, Camberwell, Victoria 3124, Australia
Penguin Books Canada Ltd, 10 Alcorn Avenue, Toronto, Ontario, Canada M4V 3B2
Penguin Books India (P) Ltd, 11 Community Centre, Panchsheel Park, New Delhi - 110 017, India
Penguin Books (N.Z.) Ltd, Cnr Rosedale and Airborne Roads, Albany, Auckland, New Zealand
Penguin Books (South Africa) (Pty) Ltd, 24 Sturdee Avenue, Rosebank,
  Johannesburg 2196, South Africa

Penguin Books Ltd, Registered Offices: Harmondsworth, Middlesex, England

First published in Penguin Books 2003

10 9 8 7 6 5 4 3 2 1

All of the essays in this volume originally appeared in different form in *The New York Review of Books* with the exception of the following: the foreword and "Poetry by and for Children" were published in different form in issues of *The New York Times Book Review;* "What Fairy Tales Tell Us" in *American Fairy Tales: From Rip Van Winkle to the Rootabaga Stories,* edited by Neil Philip, Hyperion Books, and *The Oxford Book of Modern Fairy Tales,* edited by Alison Lurie, Oxford University Press; and "Louder Than Words: Children's Book Illustrations" in *The New York Times Book Review* and *Fairy Tale Illustration from Doré to Disney,* The Folio Society, London. "Enchanted Forests and Secret Gardens: Nature in Children's Literature" is published for the first time in this collection.

LIBRARY OF CONGRESS CATALOGING-IN-PUBLICATION DATA
Lurie, Alison.
    Boys and girls forever / Alison Lurie.
      p.   cm.
    Includes bibliographical references.
    ISBN 0-14-200252-6
      1. Children's stories, English—History and criticism.   2. Children's stories,
    American—History and criticism.   3. Andersen, H. C. (Hans Christian),
    1805–1875—Criticism and interpretation.   4. Children—Books and reading.   I. Title.
PR830.C513 L87 2003
820.9'9282—dc21   2002030815

Printed in the United States of America
Set in Garamond Light/Designed by Alice Sorensen

For Alexander, Susanna, and Wells Bishop

❧ CONTENTS

ꕤ FOREWORD

I T often seems that the most gifted authors of books for children are not like other writers: instead, in some essential way, they are children themselves. There may be outward signs of this condition: these people may prefer the company of girls and boys to that of adults; they read children's books and play children's games and like to dress up and pretend to be someone else. They are impulsive, dreamy, imaginative, unpredictable.

This is true of many of the writers discussed in this book, and also of other famous children's authors. E. Nesbit devoted weeks to building a toy town out of blocks and kitchenware, and wrote a story, *The Magic City*, about it. James Barrie spent his summer holidays playing pirates and Indians with the four Davies boys, and Lewis Carroll was stiff and shy among adults but relaxed and charming with children. Today, Laurent deBrunhoff, who has continued his father's Babar series for many years and is now over seventy, still climbs trees with youthful skill and delight.

Like some children, the authors of classic children's books may also prefer the company of animals to that of adults; they identify with animals and sometimes imagine themselves as dogs or cats or horses or wild birds and beasts. Beatrix Potter, the author of *Peter Rabbit*, refused to dance with eligible young men at the society balls her parents took her to, and spent most of her time with pets of every sort. T. H. White, who wrote *The Sword in the Stone*, avoided human society almost all his life. He lived alone with his hawks and his hounds, and the death of his Irish setter, Brownie, left him utterly desolate.

It is interesting to note that most of these gifted grown-up children, perhaps the majority, are British or American, just as so many of the best-loved children's books are British or American. Other nations have produced a single brilliant classic or series: Denmark, for instance, has Andersen's tales; Italy has Pinocchio, France has Babar, Finland has Moomintroll. A list of famous children's books in English, however, could easily take up a page in this volume.

Why should this be so? One explanation may be that in Britain and America more people never quite grow up. They may sometimes put on a show of maturity, but secretly they remain children, longing for the pleasures and privileges of childhood that once were theirs. And there are good reasons for them to do so. In most countries there is nothing especially wonderful about being a child of school age. For the first four or five years boys and girls may be petted and indulged, but after that they are usually expected to become little adults as soon as possible: responsible, serious, future-oriented. But in English-speaking nations, ever since the late eighteenth century, poets and philosophers and educators have maintained that there is something wonderful and unique about childhood: that simply to be young is to be naturally good and great. It may be no coincidence that the romantic glorification of youth of the sixties and early seventies was most evident in America and Britain, or that when they want to make an especially touching appeal to voters, American politicians always speak of "our kids."

Because childhood is seen as a superior condition, many Americans and Britons have been naturally reluctant to give it up. They tend to think of themselves as young much longer, and cling to childhood attitudes and amusements. On vacation, and in the privacy of their homes, they readily revert to an earlier age, and when they write, they often take the side of children against adults. As I suggested in an earlier collection of essays,[1] their books are, in the deepest sense, subversive. As writers, they make fun of adults and expose adult pretensions and failings; they suggest, subtly or otherwise, that children are braver, smarter, and more interesting than grown-ups, and that grown-up rules are made to be broken.

Today, what many authorities in the field seem to prefer are stories in which children are helped by and learn from grown-ups. The lesson may be practical or moral; the adult may be a teacher, a relative, a neighbor, a stranger, a witch or wizard, and sometimes even an alien. These kind, wise figures may not appear very often in the story, but the plot turns on their advice or example, and the happy ending wouldn't be possible without them. From Marmee in Alcott's *Little Women* to P. L. Travers's Mary Poppins, E. B. White's Charlotte, and Tolkien's Gandalf, these admirable characters guide and care for the younger and less experienced protagonists of the tales in which they appear.

When it comes to awards for literary excellence, the books that win tend to contain at least one Wise and Good Grown-up or Grown-up-Equivalent. Back in the 1950s and 1960s the stories were often set in the historical past (especially in pioneer and Revolutionary or Civil War America) and their child protagonists tended to be white. Since cultural diversity was discovered, the settings cover a wider range, and now they often feature Native

American, African American, Hispanic American, or Asian American children who, with adult help, face disasters, overcome obstacles, and learn to be brave, kind, and strong: in effect, to be responsible young adults.

Boys and girls, on the other hand, are not always interested in becoming responsible adults. The books they choose for themselves typically feature kids and/or animals who face dangers, have exciting and/or funny adventures, and help and instruct each other. Any adults who are important in the story are apt to be villains. If there are well-meaning parents and teachers around, they have almost no idea about what really goes on in their absence, like the mother in a classic picture-book version of the genre, Dr. Seuss's *The Cat in the Hat*.

Children also often like books that anxious adults would consider scary or immoral or both—books in which creepy things happen and there is often no poetic or any other justice. In my favorite local bookstore, the largest space on the shelves of the children's paperback section is devoted to a series by R. L. Stine known as *Goosebumps*. The first volume appeared in 1992, and at last count there were sixty-one, plus more than twenty spin-offs with titles like *The Goosebumps Monster Blood Pack* and *The Scare-a-Day Wall Calendar*. Essentially, *Goosebumps* is Edgar Allen Poe updated for contemporary children. The tone alternates between comic and creepy, and in the best tales the horrors are exaggerated versions of everyday juvenile fears and afflictions. In *The Haunted School*, for instance, a sixth-grader named Tommy finds his way into another part of the school building that has been boarded up since 1947, when an evil photographer, taking a class picture, caused all twenty-seven children to vanish.

As it turns out, the class has survived for half a century in an alternate world, which is entirely black and white, like an old photograph. Since 1947 they have never left the classroom, and by this time most of them have gone mad. A few others remain sane, but in a hopeless, gray condition that will be familiar to anyone who remembers the longest, most colorless days of their own education: days when, as they sat at their desks, they thought desperately, "This is driving me crazy. Am I doomed to sit here forever?"

If you look at the children's shelves in your local bookstore or library, one of the first things you might notice is that a large proportion of the stories are about animals. This is especially true of books for small children. In a recent count in my local bookstore, I found that well over half of the picture books had animal heroes or heroines. Even though the world the characters lived in was a human one with houses and cars and schools, the protagonists were dogs or mice or bears or rabbits. One of the most popular picture books of the twentieth century, Margaret Wise Brown's *Goodnight Moon*, is set in a "great green room" that is clearly that of a contemporary middle-class Western child. Yet, according to the illustrations, the inhabitant of the "great green room" is a rabbit, and so is the old lady knitting in the rocking chair.

Several more recent and popular series of picture books also have animal heroes that live in a human environment. Bears are a favorite: those in Elsie Homelund Minark's Little Bear Series and *The Berenstain Bears* by Stan and Jan Berenstain are human in all but appearance. They wear clothes and are clearly neighbors of Dick and Jane; they live in the same sort of middle-class suburb and have the same mild adventures: birthday parties, family vacations, the new sibling or pet, the first lost tooth, and so on. Children like these books, librarians tell me, because nothing much happens in them; they are easy to identify with and reassuring.

Even when the characters in a children's book begin as human, they sometimes turn into animals. For a parent, this may

not seem totally unexpected: many parents today sometimes
have the feeling that their children are turning into beasts—chat-
tering chimpanzees, maybe, or slovenly, lazy, greedy brown bears.
It actually happens in the inventive and wildly popular *Animorphs* series by Katherine A. Applegate. "All the kids are asking for those books; we can't keep them on the shelves," say the
clerks in one local store. Some adults, on the other hand, don't
care for the Animorphs: my niece Clarissa, who is a children's librarian, says her system won't purchase them.

The *Animorphs* books follow the preferred series pattern.
Their heroes are four junior-high-school students, two male and
two female, who are also culturally and socially diverse. Two of
them are white, but there is a sensitive, nature-loving black girl
who lives on a farm and a wisecracking Hispanic American boy
from the wrong side of the tracks. All the kids can become animals, and they can communicate telepathically when transformed. But if they don't change back in two hours, they are
stuck in that morph forever, like their friend Tobias, who in volume 1 spends too much time as a red-tailed hawk.

Though Tobias misses being human, he is of great help to
the others in their struggle against evil aliens called the Yeerks.
The Yeerks, who look like the small gray slugs that eat my toma-
toes, wish to conquer Earth. Their method is to crawl into the
ears of other beings and take over their minds. There is no outward sign that the person is possessed by a slug, except for an
occasional cold emotional falseness. Readers who remember their
own adolescence will not be too surprised to learn that several
people in the kids' world, including the assistant principal at
school, are really Yeerks. So is Jake's brother Tom, who always
does the right thing and never gets into trouble. "The Yeerks . . .
had already infiltrated human society, . . . cops and teachers and
soldiers and mayors and TV newspeople. They were everywhere. They could be anyone."[2] One appeal of these books, obviously, is that they give substance to the sense we have all had

at some time—perhaps most often in early adolescence—that some people, especially authority figures, are phony. The things they do and say seem false and artificial; very possibly they are under the control of evil alien forces.

Another great attraction of the *Animorphs* books is that they provide thrilling, scientifically convincing descriptions of what it might be like to be an animal. (The idea is not new: several famous earlier instances occur in T. H. White's *The Sword in the Stone*, where the wizard Merlin turns the future King Arthur into a variety of beasts, including a hawk, a fish, a hedgehog, and a snake.) The four friends have a wonderful time in their morphs; they are happiest as birds, but almost any change is fun. Since they are independent American kids, however, the one "morph" that freaks them out is the change into ants, which turn out to have no individuality but are only cells of a colony. As one of the heroes puts it, that experience was "gross beyond belief."[3]

Almost every species of animal has replaced humans in one children's book or another, though the more unusual species tend to be somewhat altered and anthropomorphized in the illustrations as well as the text. Marc Brown's Arthur began, in *Arthur's Nose* (1976), as a fairly strange-looking character. He was identified as an aardvark; he was coffee-colored and had a self-image problem: he hated his long nose. But over time Arthur has gradually undergone what my niece the librarian calls "a Michael Jackson makeover." He is now pale orange and has no visible nose, and the word *aardvark* is no longer used. Moreover, he has gone on television: at one point he had his own series on PBS.

Of course Arthur is not the only children's book hero to move into media and merchandising. What are called "tie-ins" are now the rule for popular series. Readers of *Goosebumps*, for instance, are solicited to log onto its Web site, join its fan club, and purchase T-shirts, backpacks, lunch boxes, videos, and glow-in-the-dark pens. *Animorphs* too has a Web site, and its fan club and T-shirts cannot be far behind. Maybe our children are not turning into beasts after all; instead they're turning into relentless consumers—which may be just as frightening.

This book would not have existed without the help and encouragement of many people. I am especially indebted to Barbara Epstein, the brilliant coeditor of the *New York Review of Books*, where most of these essays originally appeared in an earlier version, and to my kind and gifted agent, Melanie Jackson. Thanks too to Angelica Carpenter and the other members of the International Wizard of Oz Club who shared their centennial meeting and their expertise with me.

I should also like to thank the students in my Cornell classes on folklore and children's literature for their intelligent and perceptive comments on many of the books discussed here.

My niece Clarissa Cooke, who is a children's librarian in Manhattan, and the staffs of my favorite bookstores in Ithaca, New York (The Bookery), and Key West, Florida (Lauriat's), provided invaluable information on current reading tastes. My grandchildren, Alex, Susanna, and Wells Bishop, to whom this book is dedicated, gave me firsthand experience of what children really want to read or hear read aloud.

Finally, I am most grateful to my husband, Edward Hower, who suggested that I collect these essays into a book and made many fine suggestions for their improvement.

BOYS
AND GIRLS
& FOREVER

THE UNDERDUCKLING:
HANS CHRISTIAN ANDERSEN

I n "The Ugly Duckling"—which generations of readers have recognized as an allegory of Hans Christian Andersen's own life—the unattractive, awkward, lowborn hero becomes a swan without any effort on his part. That ending, more than anything else in the story, makes it a fantasy. Andersen began life as one of the most gawky and disadvantaged ducks that ever waddled out of a mud pond. But he transformed himself into a swan only partially, and by long and exhausting effort.

From his earliest years as the son of a dreamy, improvident cobbler and a half-illiterate washerwoman in a small Danish town, he was what would now be called a freak. He was tall and thin and clumsy; he seldom played with other children, and his greatest delight, he wrote later, "was in making clothes for my dolls."[1]

Andersen's odd appearance was not just a childhood affliction. When he was in his sixties, a traveling companion described him as

. . . strange and bizarre in his movements and carriage. His arms and legs were long and thin and out of all proportion, his hands were broad and flat, and his feet of . . . gigantic dimensions. . . . His nose [was] so disproportionately large that it seemed to dominate his whole face.[2]

Andersen was aware that he looked peculiar; as his most recent biographer, Jackie Wullschlager, tells us, he described himself in a letter to Charles Dickens as "one who seemed to have fallen from the skies."[3] He was suggesting that he was a kind of otherworldly phenomenon, part child, part fool, and part natural philosopher—what at the time was called a "mooncalf."

Andersen was never a fool, and only occasionally a philosopher, but in a sense he remained a child all his life, with a child's egotism and a child's intense and volatile emotions. In the language of today's psychology, he was acutely bipolar. He was often either wild with joy or in deep despair, wishing that he were dead. As he wrote at twenty-nine, "My pain is crushing when I suffer, but my joy when I'm happy is also inexpressible."[4] He also had a child's naive but penetrating view of adult pretension and self-deception, like the little boy at the end of "The Emperor's New Clothes," who exlaims that the ruler has nothing on.

Also, like a child, Andersen saw everything in the world as alive and conscious. In his stories not only animals and birds, but also bugs and toys and flowers and even household objects have complex human personalities. In one of his tales a saucepan and a bunch of matches relate their life stories, and an earthenware pitcher proposes that they "have an intellectual entertainment."[5] In another tale a "decent, respectable Old Street Lamp" who is about to be retired reflects on her life. She "felt very much as a superannuated ballet-dancer feels when she is dancing for the last time, and knows that to-morrow and ever after she will sit alone in her attic chamber, morning, noon, and night, unthought of and uncared for by the generous public."[6]

For Andersen, like his Street Lamp, public attention was essential. When he was thirteen, a troupe of traveling actors came to town, and Andersen somehow convinced the manager of the theater to give him a walk-on part. To his mind, he was the center of the production. "I was always the first there, put on the red silk costume, spoke my line and believed that the whole audience thought only of me," he wrote later.[7]

From an early age Andersen sought out those who could help him toward the fame he craved. He wrote letters to well-known people and called on them, begging them to listen to him sing and recite poems and stories. Anyone who has ever been in a play or published a book will recognize the type—the awkward, odd-looking, self-conscious, very young man or woman who hangs about after the show or the reading, demanding attention, insisting on reciting a speech for you, singing a song, or showing you their half-baked, over-iced poems and stories. It is often clear from the manner of these people that they are convinced they are geniuses, and are in fact doing you a favor.

The surprising thing is that once in a while someone like this is in fact a genius. This was the case with Hans Christian Andersen; but for a long time no one agreed with him. From childhood on he was convinced of his own remarkable gifts, but by the age of thirty he had failed as a singer, a dancer, and an actor. He had managed to make a thin sort of living by writing poetry and accounts of his travels in Denmark, Germany, and Italy; his sentimental novel, *Only a Fiddler,* about a poor Italian boy who achieves fame as a singer was praised by some critics. If his life had ended then, no one would have remembered him. But instead, almost by accident, he discovered his true calling as a teller of fairy stories for children.

Today, this is a legitimate occupation: successful children's writers are world famous and often very rich. But in Denmark in Andersen's day, children's literature was moralistic and drab, and fairy tales were published only by scholars.[8] When Andersen wrote his first tales in 1835, he would probably have known the collections of Jacob and Wilhelm Grimm in Germany, and their Danish follower, Matthias Winther, whose *Danish Folk Tales* had appeared in 1823.

Unlike the Grimms and Winther, however, Andersen did not just write down the stories he had heard as a child from his mother and grandmother; he went on to compose new tales of his own. And even when he retold an existing story, he made dramatic changes. In "The Tinderbox," for instance, the Princess marries the soldier at the end not because she loves him, but for practical reasons: her parents are dead, and "she liked [being queen] much better than living a prisoner in the copper palace."[9]

The heroes and heroines in the Grimms' tales and other traditional collections usually meet their reward on earth: they kill the giant, rescue the prince or princess, win a kingdom, and live happily ever after. By contrast, many of Andersen's stories end unhappily. In my collection of forty-eight of his best-known stories, twenty finish with a death, though sometimes the character who dies is rewarded by eternal life. After Andersen's Little Match Girl perishes of the cold, for instance, the spirit of her grandmother carries her off to Paradise.

In a few of his best stories, however, Andersen provides a happy ending. Little Gerda, in "The Snow Queen," rescues Kai from the icy palace of the enchantress, where his heart has been frozen solid and he spends all day trying to fit sharp flat pieces of ice together in what Andersen calls "the ice-puzzle of reason." When Gerda, weeping, embraces him, the ice in his heart dissolves, and they fall into each other's arms.

Yet mutual romantic love is very rare in Andersen's tales. Again and again, his protagonists are rejected by those they court—and in this they share the unhappy experience of their author. All his life, Andersen continually fell in love with upperclass or titled persons, both male and female. Though he made many acquaintances, he had almost no romantic success: these people liked having him come to their houses, tell stories to their children, and sign books, but their attitude always remained one of friendly, slightly distant patronage. For years he tried, often in the most embarrassing manner, to get Edvard Collin, the handsome son of his first important patron in Copenhagen, to call him by the familiar pronoun "Du"; Edvard continued to refuse, remarking that though it was a trivial thing, he had "an innate dislike" of it, similar to the dislike a woman he knew felt for wrapping paper "so much that she was sick whenever she saw it. . . . When someone whom I respect and like and have known a long time, asks me to say 'Du,' then this nasty and inexplicable feeling surfaces within me."[10]

Andersen never really recovered from this chilly rebuff, nor from the rejection he received from many other young, beautiful, and aristocratic people. Yet he continued setting his sights unreasonably high; sometimes it seems as if what he really wanted was a hopeless romantic love. Occasionally he altered facts to put a better spin on these events, declaring that he had never loved the person involved, or that circumstances, rather than their own feelings, had separated them. When he was twenty-five, he fell in love simultaneously with two siblings, Christian Voight and his sister Riborg, the children of a wealthy merchant. Riborg was already secretly engaged to a man her parents disapproved of, which may have been part of the attraction. After Riborg turned him down, he told friends that she didn't mean anything to him, but he later wrote to Edvard with a more romantic version of the story:

> . . . last summer I met a rich, lovely, spirited girl who feels the same for me as I do for her . . . certain circumstances made her marry a man who took her fortune.[11]

The emphasis on wealth in this statement leaves rather a bad taste in the mouth, and suggests that Andersen may not have felt any more real passion for Riborg than she felt for him; "certain circumstances" was a euphemism for the fact that she was in love with the other man. When, toward the end of his life, Andersen did manage to establish a happy but short-lived sexual relationship, it was with a young man.

The heroes of Andersen's tales are no more successful romantically than he was, and often for the same reasons: they aspire to union with persons or objects of a higher social class. The cardboard dancer in "The Steadfast Tin Soldier" pays no attention to the protagonist, and in "The Top and the Ball," the Top's proposal of marriage is scorned by the Ball, "who was made of morocco leather, and fancied herself a very fashionable young lady."[12]

A recurrent theme in Andersen's tales is social snobbery and social ambition. Even inanimate objects feel it: the Darning-needle tries to pass herself off as a Sewing-needle, and the Buckwheat considers himself superior to all the other plants in the field. Andersen too was obsessed with the idea of rising in society. All his life he would seek out rich and titled people, the richer and more titled the better, and he spent some of his happiest moments as the guest of royalty. He spent months traveling among small German kingdoms, staying with one royal family after another, and entertaining them and their children by telling stories. His friends back in Copenhagen did not always approve of this. When he wrote to Jonas Collin, boasting "that while he was ignored at home, Berlin high society gathered round him," Jonas was unimpressed. According to Andersen's current biographer, he wrote back saying "what an empty life, he didn't care to crawl about on the floor with the children of dukes, wasn't Andersen going to write anything?"[13]

One thing that makes Andersen's weaknesses and faults forgivable is that from his earliest years he was aware of them. "My nasty vanity sneaks in," he wrote to a friend from the awful boarding school to which he was sent at nineteen by well-meaning patrons who wanted him to receive a proper conventional education. "[T]here is a kind of unpleasant dreaminess in me, something restless and impulsive in my soul. . . ."[14]

Andersen was also able to take a humorous attitude toward his own character. As he became more successful he developed a passion for travel, most often to warmer countries where he was already famous; and he indulged this passion constantly in spite of his continuing hypochondria and anxiety. When he was on the road, he was often seasick and consumed by fears of dogs and brigands; he had the obsessive idea that one of his fellow travelers might be crazy and planning to murder him. He recognized the irrationality of all this, though he could not overcome it. "Oh, how good I am at finding things to worry about," he once wrote in his diary.[15]

Jackie Wullschlager's extensive examination of this strange, deeply self-conscious writer and his work is a remarkable achievement: thoughtful, comprehensively researched, and wonderfully readable. Ms. Wullschlager spent many months in Denmark; she was able to read Andersen's tales and letters and journals in the original, and correct earlier translations. Her comments on the meaning of the stories, and their relation to his life, are often fascinating—and so is the impression her book gives of her own feelings about Andersen.

Biographers, who necessarily spend many years in the imaginary company of their subjects, usually end up even more devoted to them then they were at first. Yet Wullschlager's book sometimes gives the impression that as time went on she became more and more exasperated with Andersen. She portrays him as deeply annoying, vain, and egotistic, suffering from "wild imagination, inner rage, tormenting anxieties and hypochondria, insatiable ambition."[16] But she also gives him credit for his charm, brilliance, originality, and—perhaps most striking of all to the reader who knows Andersen only through his works—his sophisticated self-knowledge.

As a writer, Wullschlager has some of Andersen's own down-to-earth originality and humor. When she describes Copenhagen as Andersen would have seen it for the first time at fourteen, when he left home to make his fortune, she remarks that the city "still had the layout of a fortress. . . . Within, the buildings were forced upwards like asparagus and arranged like flowerpots on a ledge."[17]

Wullschlager attributes much of Andersen's insatiable ambition to the loneliness and persecution he suffered as an ugly, clumsy, effeminate child who was teased and bullied by other children and ashamed of his family. All his life he was painfully aware not only of his mother's drinking, but of the fact that his aunt kept a whorehouse and his uncle was in the local insane asylum. And though he gloried in the role of the poor boy who becomes rich and famous, he had a lifelong dread that these shameful connections would resurface. In Denmark, where some of his history was known, and not all his books were praised by the critics, he seldom felt properly appreciated and safe. As he grew older he began to turn against his native land. From Paris, he wrote to a friend in Copenhagen, with characteristic exaggeration:

> Here, in this big strange city, Europe's most famous and noble personalities fondly surround me, . . . and at home boys sit spitting at my heart's dearest creation! . . . The Danes are evil, cold, satanic—a people well suited to the wet, mouldy-green island. . . . my home has sent me a fever from its cold, wet forests, which the Danes gaze upon and believe they love; but I don't believe in love in the North, but in evil treachery.[18]

Though he became world famous in his lifetime, Andersen's ambition was never quite satisfied. In a sense it never could be. As his biographer says, "Even after he was famous and secure, his need for constant recognition and praise was pathological, and he craved admiration like a shot of an addictive drug."[19] Andersen, of course, knew this about himself. "My name is gradually starting to shine, and that is the only thing I live for. . . . I covet honour in the same way as a miser covets gold,"[20] he admitted in a letter.

Jackie Wullschlager praises Andersen because, she believes, "he gave voice . . . to groups which had traditionally been mute and oppressed—children, the poor, those who did not fit social or sexual stereotypes."[21] It is true that in some of Andersen's tales disadvantaged persons, animals, and objects receive attention and sympathy. But very often their one-down position is also their downfall. If they aspire to higher status, and especially to union with higher-status people, animals, or objects, they are usually disappointed. The Fir Tree dreams of glory as a Christmas tree, but when he achieves this it does not satisfy him. "It must be that something still greater, still more splendid, must happen—but what?"[22] the Fir Tree muses; and he ends up dead on a rubbish heap.

It is true that Andersen's Ugly Duckling becomes a swan, and is welcomed by the other swans, but in his case heredity takes precedence over environment. As Andersen put it in his story, "It matters not to have been born in a duck-yard, if one has been hatched from a swan's egg."[23]

Although Andersen wrote more than 150 tales, only a handful of them are usually reprinted in collections for children. There is a good reason for this: though some of his stories are brilliant and moving, most are sad, distressing, or even terrifying. As a child I was frightened and upset by many of them, especially those in which a little girl misbehaves and is horribly punished. The crime that seemed to cause the most awful result was vanity, and it was always little girls who met this fate, never little boys. In "The Red Shoes," for instance, Karen thinks of her new morocco-leather shoes even when she is in church, and as a result she is condemned to dance in them to exhaustion; she is only saved from death when she asks the local executioner to chop off her feet with his axe. Even worse in some ways was "The Girl Who Trod on a Loaf." In this tale a "proud and arrogant" child called Inger also comes to grief because of love of her new shoes. In order to keep them clean, she throws a loaf of bread into the mud for a stepping-stone. As a result of this wasteful but trivial act, Inger and her shoes sink down into the dark, muddy marsh, where she finds herself in a foul-smelling cave

> filled with noisome toads and slimy snakes. Little Inger fell among all this horrid living filth; it was so icy cold that she shuddered from head to foot, and her limbs grew quite stiff. The loaf stuck fast to her feet and it drew her down. . . .

Long years pass, and Inger only escapes from the toads and snakes after a good old woman, on her deathbed, remembers hearing Inger's story as a child and pities her.

I was also deeply disturbed by one of Andersen's most famous tales, "The Little Mermaid," in which the heroine gives up her voice and agrees that every step she takes will feel like walking on knives, so as to have the chance of attracting the love of a prince whom she first saw at his birthday party on board a ship. When he finds the Little Mermaid on the seashore, dressed only in her long green hair, he adopts her as a kind of pet. But, like the wellborn young men and women whom Andersen loved, he does not think of her as a romantic partner, and marries a princess. The mermaid dies of grief; but after death she is transfigured, and joins the spirits of the air who "fly invisibly through the dwellings of men, wherever there are children."

Though the Little Mermaid was presented as romantically admirable, I took her story as a warning against self-sacrificial and hopeless love. I did not realize that in this tale Andersen had foretold his own future. He would be rejected again and again by those he loved most, but unlike the Little Mermaid he never gave up his voice, and the best of the stories he told would survive for hundreds of years, "wherever there are children."

LITTLE WOMEN AND BIG GIRLS: LOUISA MAY ALCOTT

A hundred and sixteen years after its publication, Louisa May Alcott's *Little Women* was a smash hit again. The new film version set records (mainly, as one might expect, among women of various sizes), and the book, which has never been out of print, sold even more copies than usual. And at Orchard House, the Alcott homestead in Concord, Massachusetts, mobs of tourists created what were described as chaotic conditions.

In some quarters *Little Women* was also welcomed for its support of what are called "Christian family values." After all, it is the story of a united and affectionate family living in a small New England town that has become part of the American myth. It features kind, wise, and loving parents, always ready with a warm hug and a moral lesson, and four charming teenage daughters who have never heard of punk rock or crack cocaine. Moreover, the book is American history as well as myth: it is based on Alcott's own childhood and adolescence.

One era's conservatism, however, may be the liberal protest of an earlier time. When it appeared in 1869, *Little Women* was in many ways a radical manifesto. Its author was an independent, self-supporting single woman in an age when, as Meg puts it in the book, "men have to work and women to marry for money."[1] More than forty years before women got the vote, Louisa May Alcott was a committed feminist who wrote and spoke in favor of women's rights. In 1868, while she was creating *Little Women*, she joined the New England Suffragist Association.

Alcott came by her radicalism naturally. She was the daughter of what would now be described as vegetarian hippie intellectuals with fringe religious and social beliefs, and she spent nearly a year of her childhood in an unsuccessful commune. Her most famous book, *Little Women*, was equally radical in its time. Its central character, Jo March, has almost nothing in common with the suffering, self-sacrificing heroines of the bestselling girls' books of the day—books like Charlotte Yonge's *The Daisy Chain* (1856) and Susan Warner's *The Wide, Wide World* (1861), both of which Jo reads in the course of the novel.

Developments in intellectual and social history, and even in human biology, have greatly altered the impact of *Little Women*. The unaffected asexual innocence of the four teenage March sisters, for instance, now seems almost unbelievable. In fact it would be inconceivable today, but not in 1868. Louisa May Alcott wasn't portraying herself and her sisters as unnaturally immature, but as typical adolescents of a time when most women did not reach puberty until their late teens. In England, where the best records exist, the median age of menarche (first menstruation) in the 1830s was 17.5; by the 1860s it had fallen only to 16.5, and by the 1890s to 15.5. (Today it is down to 12.5.)[2] A young woman born in the 1830s (like Louisa May Alcott and her sisters) who married at sixteen or seventeen, as many did, might be barely sexually mature at the time of the wedding.

Several explanations have been offered for this delay in maturation. The most common is that it was due to deficiencies in women's diet, and to their lack of exercise. In the early nineteenth century it was generally believed that middle- and upper-class women needed different food than men did: more sugar and much less protein. The meals in *Little Women* emphasize sweets and carbohydrates: biscuits, pancakes, lemonade, gingerbread, pudding, fruit in season—and for a treat, ice cream, cake, and coffee. Meat and vegetables are hardly mentioned. Middle-class nineteenth-century women were also much less active than men, and the voluminous, constricting clothes they wore often made it difficult for them to exercise at all.

The typical early Victorian girl in fiction is almost totally innocent and without sexual drive. Her childlike modesty and timid tremulousness when approached even by a likable suitor can be seen as instinctive rather than flirtatious; it might be compared to the reaction of a ten-year-old today to the teasing of boy playmates.

Part 1 of *Little Women*, though it is set in the years of the Civil War (1860–64), was actually based on Louisa's own adolescence during the late 1840s. When the book begins, Amy is twelve, Beth thirteen, Jo fifteen, and Meg sixteen; none of them appear erotically mature, though Meg is on the verge. Like a ten-year-old today, they are uninterested in boys except as pals, and in no hurry to leave home. When a suitable young man falls in love with Meg, Jo calls this "a *dreadful* state of things"[3] and exclaims, "I just wish I could marry Meg myself, and keep her safe in the family."[4] The vehement childishness of this speech has puzzled some modern readers, and even led others to accusations of an unnatural lesbian attachment, but at the time it would have been seen as a comically outspoken expression of family loyalty.

Radical though she was, to some extent Louisa May Alcott softened and conventionalized her story for contemporary tastes. Her father, Bronson Alcott, was not, like Mr. March, a mild and kindly minister—he was a famous, and famously difficult, New England eccentric: unworldly, reserved, and emotionally unstable.

Mr. Alcott, the self-educated friend of Emerson and Thoreau, allowed his wife, Abba, and later his daughters (especially Louisa) to support him while he traveled about lecturing in a high-flown but fuzzy manner on transcendentalist philosophy and educational reform. For a while the family lived in a utopian community called Fruitlands, where Abba and the older girls not only did all the domestic work but served as farm laborers, while Mr. Alcott wrote high-minded accounts of the enterprise.

Bronson Alcott was not only a social radical, but a religious one as well. He was drawn to what at the time were extreme beliefs: he was an abolitionist and a vegetarian, and supported the temperance movement. His educational ideas, based on the writings of Rousseau, were far ahead of his time. The Temple School in Boston, which he founded, had to close after three years when parents objected to the admission of a black pupil and to lectures that denied the divinity of Christ. In *Little Women* Jo is familiar with the religious radicalism of her time and troubled by it. One thing her future husband, Professor Bhaer, does for her is to restore her faith:

> Somehow, as he talked, the world got right again to Jo; the old beliefs, that had lasted so long, seemed better than the new; God was not a blind force, and immortality was not a pretty fable, but a blessed fact. She . . . wanted to clap her hands and thank him.[5]

Louisa May Alcott solved the problem of her peculiar and unconventional father by largely removing him from *Little Women*. When part 1 begins, Mr. March is working at an army hospital in Washington, something Louisa herself (but not Bronson Alcott) actually did. He does not return until almost the last chapter. In part 2 he is almost as absent: "a quiet, studious man,"[6] who appears only now and then to make moral observations and criticize Jo's moneymaking sensational tales, while accepting the money they earn.

Though Bronson Alcott was unable to attract many followers or make Fruitlands a success, his daughter gave his educational and social theories wide circulation in her books. But she presented these then very radical ideas with such skill and charm that most of her readers did not protest. In *Little Women*, for instance, the girls read the New Testament and model their lives on *Pilgrim's Progress*, but do not go to church. Like the Alcott family, they never touch alcohol.

The Marches also practice charity in a hands-on way. Instead of withdrawing uneasily from the rush of German immigrants (thousands of whom flooded into America in the 1860s and 1870s), they take on the Hummel family and its seven children as a personal responsibility. Later, with the approval of her parents, Jo marries a middle-aged and penniless German with a strong accent. To understand this in contemporary terms, one must imagine the reaction of a New England WASP family whose twenty-five-year-old daughter has just announced her engagement to an unemployed Central American refugee in his forties, with two orphan nephews to support.

Alcott also conventionalized her mother and sisters to some degree. Meg, like Anna, ends up as a housewife and the mother of twins; and Beth, like Elizabeth, dies young. But Abba Alcott, who once rebelled against her husband by walking out of his commune and taking her daughters with her, becomes Marmee, a model of the patient and dutiful wife. Jo and Amy (May) were given less independence and more romantic destinies than their originals. Amy marries Laurie when she is twenty-one, and gives up art as a career because "talent isn't genius."[7] In reality May Alcott did not marry until she was over forty, after many years as a professional artist. Louisa never married, but Jo gets an unconventional but likable husband who, as Sarah Elbert says in *A*

Hunger for Home, "has all the qualities Bronson Alcott lacked: warmth, intimacy, and a tender capacity for expressing his affection."[8] He also does the shopping and shares child care.

From a mid-nineteenth-century perspective *Little Women* is both a conservative and a radical novel. Some aspects of it, and some characters, represent the past; others look to the future. Like much earlier juvenile literature, it is often sentimental, full of moral lessons, and centers on a self-contained family unit that tends to exclude outsiders. The March girls, unlike teenagers today, apparently have no close friends, and neither does Marmee. When Laurie appears, he is accepted as an adopted brother. But in an age of patriarchal Victorian families, the Marches are a matriarchy. Mr. March remains a background figure even when he is on the scene; it is Marmee to whom the girls go with their troubles, and it is she who comforts and advises them, and is the central force in the household, as is clear from the picture of the four girls grouped around her that appears in most editions—and in the advertisement for the latest film version.

In an innovation that was widely copied later, Louisa May Alcott replaced the single central character of the standard juvenile with four heroines, each with a different personality. Before *Little Women* there was one ideal type of girlhood in most American juvenile literature: modest, dutiful, and obedient. Alcott suggested that there was a range of possibilities, and also that a heroine could have serious faults—vanity, jealousy, sloth, or anger—and still earn a happy ending.[9] Moreover, through her four heroines she was able to represent and comment on four important contemporary views of womanhood.

Beth is the typical early Victorian girl-child: sweet, shy, passive, and domestic—the traditional "angel in the house." At thirteen she still plays with dolls. Her life is centered in the family, and her dearest wish for the future is "to stay at home safe with

Father and Mother."[10] Unlike the other girls, she does not work outside the home, and seems almost never to leave it. Her death, like that of Dickens's Little Nell and many other children in nineteenth-century popular fiction, suggests that innocence and virtue are innately fragile and fleeting, unable to survive in the real world. Historically speaking, Beth represents a view of womanhood that was literally passing away at the time. The hidden message to the reader is that to stay at home safe with your parents is to die.

Meg, on the other hand, is a woman of the mid–nineteenth century: an exemplar of what at the time was called the Domestic Movement. *Little Women* begins during the first winter of the Civil War, which removed men from the home and gave middle-class women like Marmee and her daughters more power and responsibility. After the war ended, many writers encouraged women to keep what they had won: to take charge of their homes and children rather than cede control to servants and male authority. That this was in many ways a new idea is clear from the episode in which the four girls try living for a week without household help, and it turns out that none of them, not even the domestic Beth, know how to cook—something that would be considered most peculiar today. Meg goes into marriage without many domestic skills, but by the end of the novel she is fully in control of her own household. If you marry and have children, the book suggests, make sure you are in charge of your own life.

Amy, the youngest Little Woman, appropriately embodies one of the newest developments in American society: the entry of women into the arts. She belongs to the generation of painters like Mary Cassatt (1845–1926) who went to Europe to study art just as their brothers had been doing for years. Amy's talent is recognized early, and though she doesn't become a professional artist, she continues to paint and sculpt, and there is no suggestion that her efforts are frivolous. Implicitly, her career suggests to the reader that if you wish "to be an artist and go to Rome," it may happen.

After her marriage to Laurie, Amy travels in Europe and together with her husband brings back artistic treasures and helps struggling artists of both sexes. She thus also stands for the many well-to-do late-nineteenth-century women like Isabella Stewart Gardner (1840–1924), May Alcott's near-contemporary, who became important collectors and patrons of the arts.

Jo, of course, represents the feminist movement; in the phrase of the period, she is a New Woman, who chooses a career. Jo is also the first and the most famous positive example in fiction of a new kind of girl: the tomboy. In chapter 1 of the book she declares, "I like boys' games and work and manners! I can't get over my disappointment in not being a boy."[11] She hates her given name of Josephine, and, as some readers have pointed out, has a nickname that might easily belong to a boy, while her friend and neighbor Theodore Laurence is known by the girlish name of Laurie. All through the book her friends and relatives keep trying to suppress the boyish side of Jo, but they never totally succeed, and at the end she is still romping about, careless of her clothes, and talking boys' slang, although she is married and a mother.

The life history Alcott gives Jo in *Little Women* and its two sequels, *Little Men* (1871) and *Jo's Boys* (1886), is well ahead of its time. In contemporary terms, she has it all: not only a husband and children but two careers; and she doesn't have to do her own housework and cooking. She gets away with it partly because both her occupations are "women's work": running a progressive boarding school and writing for children.[12] The message to the reader is clear: demand freedom and independence, and you may very well get it—and love as well.

Perhaps Jo also manages to have it all because she, like Louisa May Alcott, depreciates her literary efforts and excuses them as financially necessary. Even nearly twenty years later, in

Jo's Boys, she speaks of herself as a "literary nursery-maid who provides moral pap for the young."[13]

Louisa May Alcott, like many women writers of her time, put her duty to help support her family above the demands of art, and felt under pressure to write as fast as possible. Of one of her best adult novels, *Work* (1865), she wrote, "Not what it should be—too many interruptions. Should like to do one book in peace and see if it wouldn't be good."[14] But although she was supplying her parents with a very comfortable lifestyle and sending her sister to study in Europe, she never allowed herself to "do one book in peace."

This sort of female self-destruction and self-denigration, perhaps undertaken originally out of lack of confidence, or to deflect criticism, was endemic in the late nineteenth century, and continued long into the twentieth. Possibly as a result, men gave up their exclusive rights to the production of "serious literature" very slowly. Even after they began to allow writing by females into what is now called the canon, they remained enviously reluctant to admit that a woman could produce both good books and babies. For many years the serious woman writer, if married, had to be childless like Charlotte Brontë, George Eliot, and Virginia Woolf; it was even better if she were single, like Emily Brontë and Emily Dickinson. Gifted novelists and mothers such as Elizabeth Gaskell and Margaret Oliphant were seen as somehow unimportant and second-rate; often it was implied that their books would only interest other women. Even today no mother has been admitted into the Library of America.

Though she was unmarried, Louisa May Alcott's attitude toward her own work and current critical prejudice ensured that for more than a hundred years she was dismissed as merely a juvenile author. It was not until the 1980s that her books were taken seriously and her adult novels—*Moods* (1865), *Behind a Mask* (1866), Work (1872), *A Modern Mephistopheles* (1877), and *A Whisper in the Dark* (1888)—were reread and reissued. By

1990 she was a hot property. The manuscript of her romantic novel, *A Long Fatal Love Chase*, considered too sensational for publication in her own time, was bought by Random House for $1.5 million. The actress Sharon Stone was also said to be "practically obsessed" by the idea of starring in a film version. Unfortunately, nothing seems to have come of this possibility.

Little Women has always attracted moviemakers. The 1995 film was the fifth (two silent versions have been lost), following those of 1933 and 1949. It was directed by an Australian, Gillian Armstrong (best known for her lively *My Brilliant Career*). In many ways the film is an outstanding success: the New England scenery looks real as well as picturesque, and the March family house is not ridiculously large. For the first time, the characters are not obviously wearing makeup, and their clothes appear actually to have been worn and washed and mended before they were photographed. There is even a strong family resemblance among the *Little Women:* Trini Alvarado as Meg, Winona Ryder as Jo, and Claire Danes as Beth really look like sisters, something that has never been true before.

In other ways, however, the demands of Hollywood seem to have won out over authenticity. It is easy to forgive the heightened drama of some of the scenes in the film: the invented moment when Laurie kisses the twelve-year-old Amy, and the suspense-filled last-minute meeting of Jo and Professor Bhaer. The glamorizing of the characters is harder to accept. As Anne Hollander perceptively pointed out in *The New York Times*,[15] in each film version Professor Bhaer has become younger and better-looking. In the book he is a stocky middle-aged man with thick glasses whom Jo loves in spite of his nondescript appearance: Paul Lukas, in 1933, more or less fit the part. In 1949 Rossano Brazzi was middle-aged but attractive, and in the latest version Jo ends up with the romantically handsome Gabriel Byrne.

In all three films the Hollywood demand for stars also affected the casting of the four sisters. Alcott presents Jo as definitely plain: she is "tall, thin, and brown"[16] and still coltishly awkward at sixteen, in an age when the ideal woman was petite, rounded, pink, and graceful. In the 1933 version Katherine Hepburn was not only ten years older and absolutely wonderful-looking, she obviously came from another and more aristocratic background than the rest of the family. June Allyson, who played Jo in 1949, was thirty-two and looked it. In the most recent version, Jo's long, thick chestnut hair is described, as in the book, as her "one beauty,"[17] a remark that makes no sense, since Winona Ryder was one of Hollywood's most striking young actresses.

When the book begins, Amy is twelve and in despair over her flat nose, which she tries to improve by wearing a clothespin on it. In the 1933 version she was played by Joan Blondell, who was not only very pretty but twenty-four and pregnant. In the 1949 film version of *Little Women* Amy was the seventeen-year-old Elizabeth Taylor, possibly the most perfectly beautiful teenager in America at that time, with a nose that thousands of girls would have died for. In the new film Amy is still very pretty, but at last she is a real child actress, Kirsten Dunst.

The further we are from the nineteenth century, of course, the more *Little Women* seems a period piece. The 1933 film could still present the Marches as an idealized version of the contemporary American family. By the end of the twentieth century they were clearly a vanished species. Perhaps that is why attempts were made in the recent film to update the story. The gap Louisa May Alcott created between her own life and that of her characters, for instance, was collapsed, and bits of Alcott biography and literary history were shoehorned into the film. Jo asks Professor Bhaer if he knows what transcendentalism is (he does, of course); and we are informed that Mr. March's school, like Bronson Alcott's, was closed after he admitted a black student. And Susan Sarandon (looking lovely but somewhat uncomfortable in a hoop skirt) speaks on the importance of rights for women, and against slavery and the constrictions of the corset, expressing the radical opinions of Louisa May Alcott and her mother rather than those of the more pious and proper Marmee of the book.

As usual in movies set in the American past, the film *Little Women* is wonderful to look at, full of Currier and Ives New England landscapes, picturesque nineteenth-century costumes, horse-drawn carriages, log fires, and loving relatives gathered round a Christmas dinner table or dancing on the grass at a summer wedding. It is not surprising that reactionaries should see it as propaganda for family piety, reverence for established institutions, and the domestication of women. But under its old-fashioned disguise, the film, like the book, still recommends quite another set of values.

THE ODDNESS OF OZ

THE year 2000 was the centenary of a famous and much-loved but essentially very odd children's classic: L. Frank Baum's *The Wizard of Oz*. Those who recall the story only from childhood reading, or from the MGM film, have perhaps never realized how strange the original book and its sequels are.

For one thing, the Oz books are far ahead of their time both scientifically and politically. They are full of inventions that would not appear on the market for most of the century, among them a robot man, an artificial heart and limbs, a television monitoring system, antigravity devices, and a computer-type news service. Oz is also, as several critics have noted, both a sort of socialist utopia and a deeply matriatchal and occasionally trans-sexual society.[1]

Some of the reasons for this may lie in Baum's own history—and also in that of his wife. As a child in Chittenango, New York, Frank Baum (he disliked his first name, Lyman, and never used it) did not go to school; instead he remained at home under his mother's care and was educated by tutors. But when he was

twelve, his father, a successful banker and oil executive, hoping
to toughen Frank up and cure him of his "daydreaming,"[2] sent
him to the Peekskill Military Academy. Baum was miserable
there for more than a year, and the only results of the experi-
ment were a physical (and possibly also psychological) breakdown, and a lifelong aversion to both formal education and the
military.

Back home on the family estate, Rose Lawn, Baum continued his studies. He also read widely, published a neighborhood
newspaper on his own printing press, and put on plays with his
brothers and sisters. Gradually he developed an intense and lifelong fascination with the theater, and in 1878 he began to work
as a professional actor. Four years later his father bought him a
small dramatic company, and Baum was soon adapting and star-
ring in a romantic melodrama, *The Maid of Arran*.

In 1881, when Baum was twenty-five, he fell in love with a
twenty-year-old Cornell sophomore. Maud Gage was the youngest daughter and favorite child of one of the most famous feminists in America, Matilda Gage. Together with Elizabeth Cady
Stanton and Susan B. Anthony, Matilda had just begun to publish a groundbreaking three-volume *History of Woman Suffrage*
(1881–89). She was prominent in the radical wing of the suffrage
movement, and for years had spoken out not only for women's
right to vote and the abolition of slavery, but against unrestrained
capitalism, established religion, and ethnic and racial oppres-
sion. She was especially concerned with the wrongs suffered by
Native Americans, and enthusiastic about the system of government practiced by the Iroquois Confederacy, in which men and
women were near-equals. (Eventually, in gratitude for Gage's
efforts on their behalf, the Mohawk nation adopted her into
their wolf clan and gave her the name She-Who-Holds-the-Sky.)

Matilda Gage's husband, Henry Hill Gage, appears to have
been something of a nonentity. He was a successful merchant,

able to provide his family with an impressive white-columned mansion in Fayetteville, New York; but I could find no record of what he thought of his wife's political and literary activities.

As time passed, Matilda Gage's ideas became too radical for both Anthony and Stanton, and in 1890 she was forced out of the National Woman Suffrage Association, which she had helped to found in 1869. Later she was partially written out of feminist history: a recent PBS documentary on Anthony and Stanton hardly mentioned her.

Frank Baum met Maud Gage in 1881 at a Christmas party, and he soon began calling on her and courting her. A few months later he proposed, and Maud accepted him at once, without first consulting her parents—an unusual step at the time. When Matilda Gage heard the news, she was not pleased; she exclaimed, "I won't have my daughter be a darned fool and marry an actor." Maud replied, "All right, Mother, if you feel that way about it, good-bye."[3] Faced with a stubbornness equal to her own, Matilda laughed and backed down. The couple was married in the family home in Fayetteville, near Syracuse, in November 1882, less than a year after their first meeting.

In a sense Matilda Baum was right; from a practical point of view it was a foolish marriage. It would be many years before Frank Baum began to be financially secure, and at first he failed or barely survived in one occupation after another: theater owner, newspaper editor, dry-goods merchant, traveling salesman, and trade-magazine publisher. After Baum's father lost most of his fortune and died in 1887, Frank and Maud were often on the edge of poverty. Fortunately, where Baum was dreamy, easygoing, and impractical, Maud, like her mother, was what at the time was known as a New Woman: independent, freethinking, strong willed, and clearheaded. She also had a quick temper. Later in her life she maintained that the couple had always lived in peace and harmony, but as one of Baum's early biographers reports,

. . . those who knew the family best felt that this was true only because Frank, from the time of their marriage until his death thirty-seven years later, allowed her to have her own way with the household, the children, and the family purse.[4]

After the marriage Matilda Gage and her daughter remained close, and when Baum and Maud moved to Chicago in 1891 with four small boys, Matilda came to stay with them every winter and help take care of the children. But she did far more than this for Baum. It was she who first encouraged her son-in-law to write down the tales he had been telling the neighborhood children, and send them to a publisher. According to Angela Carpenter, "Frank could not believe anyone would want his stories, but Maud said firmly, 'Mother is nearly always right about everything.'"[5] So he sent off the manuscript of his first children's book, *Mother Goose in Prose*; it was accepted at once and became a best-seller.

Possibly these events convinced Baum of the value of his mother-in-law's opinions; or perhaps he was already convinced. Earlier, when he was editing a failing newspaper in South Dakota, he published Maud Gage's "Manifesto" of women's rights, and wrote in favor of votes for women. Later, his books for children, especially the fourteen Oz books, would reflect many of Matilda Gage's most radical ideas.

Among Matilda Gage's striking and original views was her belief in a prehistoric matriarchal society, the "Matriarchate." In *Woman, Church, and State* (1895), partly written when she was living in Chicago with Baum and his family, she declared that all ancient communities had been ruled by women.

A form of society existed at an early age known as the Matriarchate or Mother-rule. Under the Matriarchate, except as son and inferior, man was not recognized in either of these great institutions, family, state or church. A father and husband as such, had no place either in the social, political or religious scheme; woman was ruler in each.[6]

In this golden age, according to Gage's biographer, Sally Rosch Wagner, "Far from woman using her power over man oppressively, Gage maintained that never was justice more perfect, never civilization higher than under the Matriarchate."[7]

Like other radical feminists in both the nineteenth and twentieth centuries, Matilda Gage believed that if women held political power the world would be a better place. Women leaders would be kind, wise, just, fair-minded, and nonviolent. Today, in an era that might be designated as AMT (After Margaret Thatcher), this belief seems naive, but at the time it was widely accepted in feminist circles. In 1915 Charlotte Perkins Gilman, a contemporary of Matilda Gage, published a fantasy novel called *Herland*, which portrays a peaceful and happy all-feminist society.

In Frank Baum's Oz, women rule all the good societies and some of the bad ones. At the start of the series the Emerald City is governed by a man, the Wizard of Oz, but it presently becomes clear that he is an incompetent phony with no magical powers. For a short time after volume 1 the Emerald City is governed by Dorothy's friend the Scarecrow, but by the end of the second volume, and for the remainder of the series, not only the capital but the entire Land of Oz has a female sovereign, Princess Ozma: a pretty little girl who began life under an enchantment as a pretty little boy.

For Matilda Gage witches were not necessarily evil. Even after the triumph of patriarchy, she maintained, some women continued to observe the beliefs and rituals of earlier times. The witches of the late medieval and early modern age, she claimed, were pagan priestesses, skilled in healing. (Gage's views on this subject, according to an excellent recent study by the British historian Ronald Hutton, *The Triumph of the Moon*, would have a formative influence on the early-twentieth-century revival of paganism and witchcraft in Britain.)

When Dorothy first arrives in Oz by cyclone, the land is divided into four countries, two governed by good witches and two by wicked ones. Ozma is aided and advised by a beautiful young woman, Glinda the Good, originally known as the Good Witch of the South. (Later, after objections from readers, Baum referred to her only as "a powerful sorceress.") Their relationship is that of a wise, affectionate mother and her daughter. Like Matilda Gage, Glinda is nearly always right about everything, and when there is a crisis she has the magical solution. Troubles and dangers occur in all of Baum's fourteen Oz books, of course: if they didn't there would be no plot. But in every case, whenever things look darkest, either Ozma or Glinda or Dorothy, or more than one of them, is there to rescue the good characters, administer justice, and restore order.

As some critics have suggested, from a religious point of view the Land of Oz is ruled by a female trinity, all of them eternally young and beautiful: Glinda, who appears to be in her early twenties; Ozma, who in *The Tin Woodman of Oz* (1918) is said to be fourteen or fifteen; and Dorothy, who is "much younger" than Ozma.[8] As in the Christian Trinity, it is the junior member of the group, Dorothy, who most often goes out into the world to help people in trouble. The senior member, on the other hand, sometimes takes a poisiton of benevolent detachment. There is an interesting scene in Baum's final book, *Glinda of Oz* (1920), in which Glinda suggests that Dorothy and Ozma should forget about the two warring kingdoms whose problems they have heard of, remarking:

"Had you not learned of the existence of the Flatheads and the Skeezers, through my Book of Records, you would never have worried about them or their quarrels. So, if you pay no attention to these peoples, you may never hear of them again."

"But that wouldn't be right," declared Ozma. "I am ruler of all the land of Oz, . . . it is my duty to make all my people— wherever they may be—happy and contented and to settle their disputes. . . ."9

In the world of Oz, at least half of the many eccentric sub-societies also have female rulers. Not all of them are benevolent, but their faults are, in early-twentieth-century terms, more feminine than masculine. Some are willful and greedy; others are vain, idle, and self-centered like Queen Coo-ee-oh in *Glinda of Oz* or Princess Languidere in *Ozma of Oz* (1907), who devotes most of her time to trying on the thirty beautiful heads she owns and admiring herself in the mirror. Here too there may be a feminist message. When the book appeared, it was just becoming possible for a respectable woman to use rouge and powder and hair dye in order to alter her appearance temporarily. But many radical feminists of the time, like those of our own era, scorned this sort of artifice, and Baum seems to have shared their views.

Dorothy, like Matilda and Maud Gage, is clearly a New Woman. Her virtues are those of a Victorian hero rather than a Victorian heroine: she is brave, active, independent, sensible, and willing to confront authority. In *Ozma of Oz* the vain Princess Languidere becomes interested in Dorothy's head:

"You are rather attractive," said the lady presently. "Not at all beautiful, you understand, but you have a certain style of prettiness that is different from that of any of my thirty heads. So I believe I'll take your head and give you No. 26 for it."

"Well, I believe you won't!" exclaimed Dorothy. . . . "I'm not used to taking cast-off things, so I'll just keep my own head."10

In *Dorothy and the Wizard of Oz* (1908) Dorothy and her cousin
Zeb are caught in an earthquake and fall through a crack in California into a magical world. Zeb is terrified, but Dorothy remains
calm, and talks back to the evil Sorcerer of the Mangaboos, un-
feeling vegetable beings covered with thorns.

> The Sorcerer . . . looked towards the little girl with cold,
> cruel eyes. . . .
>   "Why have you dared to intrude your unwelcome persons
> into the secluded Land of the Mangaboos?" he asked, sternly.
>   "Cause we couldn't help it," said Dorothy. . . .
>   "Prove it!" cried the Sorcerer.
>   "We don't have to prove it," answered Dorothy, indig-
> nantly. "If you had any sense at all you'd known it was the
> earthquake."[11]

Later Dorothy is equally unimpressed by a caveful of baby dragons who boast of their long aristocratic pedigree:

> "Well," said Dorothy, "I was born on a farm in Kansas, and I
> guess that's being just as 'spectable and haughty as living in
> a cave with your tail tied to a rock. If it isn't I'll have to stand
> it, that's all."[12]

In *The Emerald City of Oz* (1910) Dorothy comes to stay in
Oz permanently; she is made a princess and given elegant and
luxurious quarters in the palace (lovingly described by Baum,
who adored theatrical display). Yet in spite of the delights of the
Emerald City, Dorothy is soon bored and eager to go on new
adventures.

Betsy and Trot, the little American girls who are the heroines
of two later Oz books, are equally adventurous and confronta-
tional: Betsy, like Dorothy, even stands up to the evil Nome
King. After their adventures are over, they also get to stay in the
palace and are assigned jewel-trimmed suites near Dorothy's.

The only boy hero of the series, Ojo, in *The Patchwork Girl of Oz* (1913), however, receives merely "a nice house just outside the walls of the Emerald City,"[13] though his companion, the Patchwork Girl, is allowed to live in the palace.

Like Dorothy, these alternative child heroes are always accompanied by what folklorists call Animal Helpers. Baum's remarkable powers of invention are in evidence here: Betsy has her mule, Hank; and Trot has a four-legged bird with a helicopter tail, the Ork. Ojo is joined on his travels not only by the Patchwork Girl, but by a clever, coldhearted Glass Cat and a good-natured square wooden dog called the Woozy. The boy Tip, who later becomes Ozma, not only has the good-natured and tireless Sawhorse for a companion, but a strange flying creature called the Gump, who has been put together out of two sofas, a collection of feather dusters, and the stuffed head of an antelope.

One of the themes of the early feminist movement was the presentation of housework as oppressive, since it was unpaid, underappreciated, and physically exhausting—far more exhausting, of course, in an era before frozen food, washing machines, refrigerators, and vacuum cleaners, when vegetables had to be canned, clothes and floors scrubbed, ice chopped, and carpets beaten by hand. Baum seems to share this view. In the first volume of his series, *The Wizard of Oz*, the Wicked Witch of the West, as Osmond Beckwith puts it, "'tortures' Dorothy by making her do housework."[14] In *Glinda of Oz* Dorothy refuses to sweep and dust and wash dishes for The King of All Spiders, even under severe threat.

For the time this attitude, which Matilda Gage shared, was unusual, to say the least. It was common for the heroines of most nineteenth- and early-twentieth-century children's fiction to learn household skills and to enjoy them. In Louisa May Alcott's books great emphasis is put on being able to sew and mend stockings and produce tasty and nourishing meals; later the eponymous heroine of *Anne of Green Gables* (1908) learns to bake and iron and sew patchwork. Throughout Baum's series, however, his female protagonists are never instructed in the domestic arts, though ordinary women all seem to be skilled in them. Meals in Oz often grow on trees or are prepared by invisible hands. When Dorothy and her friends are not on the road having adventures, they have nothing to do but play.

In the world of the Oz books, male rulers are almost always wicked or weak or both. The Wizard of Oz's magic powers are parlor tricks, and nobody seems sad when he is deposed and leaves Oz in his balloon. Later in the series he is allowed to return and learn a little real magic under the guidance of Glinda, but it's always clear that he is only her apprentice.

Oz, of course, is full of benevolent male characters who accompany Dorothy and later child protagonists on their adventures. Most of these beings, however, are either senior citizens like the Shaggy Man and Trot's friend Cap'n Bill, or nonhuman, like the Scarecrow, the Cowardly Lion, Jack Pumpkinhead, the mechanical Tik-Tok, and the Wogglebug. They are comic figures, and often in some way damaged or incompetent; none are as brave or resourceful as his child companion. A Freudian critic has called them emasculated.[15] Only one of these nonhuman characters, the Patchwork Girl, is female, and she is remarkable for her insouciant self-confidence.

Two of Dorothy's companions, the Scarecrow and the Tin Woodman, appear to represent unfortunate extremes of male identity. The Scarecrow, who is made of cloth and straw, is too soft: he lacks a brain and can feel but not think. The metallic Tin Woodman is too hard: he lacks a heart and can think but not feel. The Tin Woodman, of course, was once a human woodcutter, but all the parts of his body have been chopped off one

after another and replaced with metal. He alone is given a kingdom to rule in *The Wizard of Oz:* he becomes the Emperor of
the Winkies, but remains subservient to Ozma. In a later book
of the series, *The Tin Woodman of Oz,* he decides to search for
his former human fiancée Nimmee Amee. He no longer loves
her, since the red silk heart he received from the Wizard of Oz
is capable of friendship but not passion:

> . . . the Wizard's stock of hearts was low, and he gave me a
> Kind Heart instead of a Loving Heart, so that I could not love
> Nimmee Amee any more than I did when I was heartless.[16]

Nevertheless, he feels obligated to offer to marry Nimmee Amee
out of duty. On the journey to find her he discovers another
metallic man, Captain Fyter, the Tin Soldier, who was also once
human and also engaged to Nimmee Amee. Neither of them
really wants the girl, and they are relieved to discover that Nimmee Amee is now married to a man called Chopfyt who has
been cobbled together out of both their old human parts. He is
less than perfect, but Nimmee Amee declares herself satisfied
with him:

> ". . . I married him because he resembled you both," [she
> says]. "I won't say he is a husband to be proud of, because
> he has a mixed nature, and isn't always an agreeable com-
> panion. But he is my husband, and I must make the best of
> him."[17]

Besides, he does housework: "He is now trained to draw the
water and carry in the wood and hoe the cabbages and weed
the flower-beds and dust the furniture."[18] She tells the Tin
Woodman and the Tin Soldier "to go back to your own homes
and forget me, as I have forgotten you."[19] Since they have by
now become close friends, they are happy to take her advice.

The dominant villain of the Oz books is the ugly little Nome King, who lives under a mountain and rules over hundreds of all-male miners and soldiers. He has childish temper tantrums, hates all happy people, and is terrified of eggs. In *Ozma of Oz* the Nome King and his vast army are put to rout by Dorothy's pet hen, Billina, who not only spies on him and discovers the secret of his magic, but supplies the other good characters liberally with her eggs. (Oddly enough, Billina, like Ozma, is a sort of transsexual. She began life as Bill, and repeatedly insists that this is her real name, though eventually she becomes the mother of many chickens who seem to have no father.)

Later, in *The Emerald City of Oz*, the Nome King forms a military alliance with three other disagreeable nations: the Whimsies, the Growleywogs, and the Phanfasms. Their purpose is to conquer the Land of Oz and enslave its inhabitants; but each of the rulers is plotting to deceive and outwit the other three and take all the spoils for himself. Presently the Nomes begin to dig a long tunnel under the Deadly Desert that protects Oz from invaders. Ozma and Glinda find out about this with the help of their superior magical technology, and fill the tunnel with dust. When the four armies emerge in the palace gardens of the Emerald City, they are dreadfully thirsty. Their first act is to drink of the Fountain of Oblivion, which causes them instantly to forget everything, including their dreams of conquest, and become like innocent children.

Unfortunately, the Nome King does not remain an innocent child for long. Perhaps because of the exigencies of plot, his evil nature reasserts itself, and he has to be defeated twice more, first in *Tik-Tok of Oz* (1914) with the help of more eggs, and then in *The Magic of Oz* (1919) by drinking the water of oblivion again.

Eggs and water are both traditional symbols of natural force and life, and thus appropriate weapons against evil, which in the Oz books is always portrayed as sterile and dehydrated. After Dorothy's house lands on the Wicked Witch of the East, killing her, her body is so dry and dusty that she simply blows away. And when Dorothy destroys the Wicked Witch of the West by throwing a bucket of water over her, she dissolves like brown sugar and can be swept out the door.

The Wizard of Oz represents a sharp break with the European nineteenth-century tradition of children's fantasy, in both style and content. This was deliberate on Baum's part. In his introduction he declared his wish to write "a modernized fairy tale" in which "the stereotyped genie, dwarf, and fairy are eliminated."[20]

Both the characters and the setting of *The Wizard of Oz* are very American. Like the protagonists of many European folktales, Dorothy is accompanied on her initial journey by three "magic helpers." But they are not the traditional magically gifted humans or enchanted beasts. The Tin Woodman was based on a figure Baum had created himself when he was decorating a hardware store window in Indiana. Scarecrows stood guard over hundreds of midwestern cornfields, and the Cowardly Lion could be seen any day moping in the Chicago zoo.

The Wizard himself, that famous humbug, with his gift for showmanship and publicity, and his lack of real powers, is a well-known American type. Not only does he resemble many of our politicians, past and present, but he also recalls the nineteenth-century traveling pitchman and sideshow barker, a type that reached its apotheosis in the impressario P. T. Barnum. Baum suggests both these connections when he reveals in later volumes that the Wizard's father was a politician, and that he himself used to be with "Bailum and Barney's Circus."

Dorothy too is recognizably American, though she has much in common with her most famous predecessor, Lewis Carroll's

Alice. Both are independent, brave, and practical little girls, but
Alice, as un upper-middle-class Victorian child, is far more concerned with manners and social status. She worries about the
proper way to address a mouse, and is glad she doesn't have to
live in a pokey little house like Mabel. Dorothy already lives in
a pokey little house, which she is deeply attached to. Demogra-
phers would class her among the rural poor, but she takes for
granted her equality with everyone she meets.

   The landscape of the Oz book too is familiar. Dorothy's
Kansas suggests Aberdeen, South Dakota, where Baum tried un-
successfully to run a general store and then a weekly newspaper between 1888 and 1891, years marked by drought, crop
failures, falling farm prices, and a disastrous cyclone. "Not a tree
nor a house broke the broad sweep of flat country that reached
the edge of the sky in all directions. The sun had baked the
plowed land into a gray mass, with little cracks running through
it. Even the grass was not green, for the sun had burned the tops
of the long blades until they were the same grey color."[21]

   Oz itself can be seen as an idealized version of America in
1900—happily isolated from the rest of the world, underpopu-
lated, and largely rural, with an expanding magic technology
and what appear to be unlimited natural resources. Its lush veg-
etation and whimsical architecture also suggest Southern California, where Baum spent his final years.

The Oz books were written at a time when racial and ethnic
prejudice was part of the cultural climate. Comedians routinely
made fun of Irish, Polish, Italian, and other immigrants, as well
as of blacks and Native Americans. Many public and private institutions were segregated, and some politicians recommended
the deportation of minorities, or their instant, enforced assimila-
tion. But Baum's mother-in-law, Matilda Gage, like other radi-
cals, protested these views.

> Unless liberty is attained [she declared in 1862, during the Civil War]—the broadest, the deepest, the highest liberty for *all*—not for one set alone, one clique alone, but for man and woman, black and white, Irish, Germans, Americans, and Negroes, there can be no permanent peace.[22]

In the world of Oz, acceptance of minority rights is taken for granted. Baum's books are full of eccentric subsocieties, some of them dangerous to outsiders. The Hammerheads, for instance, assault travelers with their huge, hard heads, which are mounted on extensible necks; the Wheelers, who resemble semihuman bicycles, attempt to run over strangers. In a single volume of the series, *Dorothy and the Wizard in Oz*, the protagonists are threatened and attacked by the coldhearted vegetable Managaboos, who grow on bushes; the invisible carnivorous bears in the Valley of Voe; and a mob of angry wooden Gargoyles, who live in a country where the ground is sawdust and the leaves of the trees are shavings. Though all these creatures cause Dorothy and her friends a great deal of trouble, it is never suggested that they should be destroyed or even reformed—instead they appear to have a right to their own peculiar customs and way of life.

The social and political system of Oz, as presented—with some inconsistencies—in the series, appears to be a compromise between Baum's own love of royalty, fancy dress, and theatrical display, and Matilda Gage's democratic socialism. Princess Dorothy and Queen Ozma and their friends live in a palace paved with marble and gold and jewels, and wear extravagant costumes; they are treated with great deference by the ordinary inhabitants. But outside the palace equality reigns. There is no money in Oz; instead all products and services are freely shared, and everyone receives whatever he or she needs. The economy is largely agricultural, and no mention is made of machinery except for Tik-Tok, the Mechanical Man, and the magical inventions monopolized by Ozma and Glinda.

A good deal of the social criticism in the Oz books seems to derive from Baum's own experiences. There is, for example, the ongoing satire on education and armies, which may be related to his unpleasant experiences at the Peekskill Military Academy. Academic authority is represented in Oz by Mr. H. M. Woggle-Bug, T. E., a huge beetle (possibly a cockroach, to judge by the illustrations). His initials, characteristic of academics a century ago even more than today, stand for Highly Magnified and Thoroughly Educated. The Woggle-Bug became trapped under a microscope in a classroom and grew to human size; before his escape, he absorbed a great deal of knowledge. Like some professors, he is extremely vain of his learning and makes terrible puns. Presently the Woggle-Bug founds a College of Athletics where students get instant education by taking pills, and can thus devote all their time to sports.

In Baum's books armies and soldiers are either serious and hateful or comic and ineffectual. The Nomes and their allies are horrifying; the Soldier With the Green Whiskers who guards the gate of the Emerald City, in spite of his handsome uniform and great height, is a coward and a ninny. The second book in the series, *The Marvelous Land of Oz* (1904), contains a famous extended satire on militant—indeed, military—feminism. Baum's mother-in-law, Matilda Gage, had died in 1898, so she could not object to—or be hurt by—the story, which suggests that however favorably disposed Baum was to feminism, he also enjoyed making fun of its political aspects. Early in *The Marvelous Land of Oz* the Emerald City is occupied by an Army of Revolt consisting of four hundred girl soldiers from each of the kingdoms of Oz, led by General Jinjur, whose pretty face "wore an expression of discontent coupled to a shade of defiance or audacity."[23] The goal of Jinjur and her army is "to obtain power over our former oppressors," that is, men.[24] When they appear, the Emerald City's one soldier runs away, and Jinjur easily achieves victory. Soon gender roles are reversed: the men are "sweeping and dusting and washing dishes, while the women sat around in groups, gossiping and laughing."[25] But Baum also gives women credit for their natural skill and endurance: as one exhausted husband complains, "doing housework and minding the children is wearing out the strength of every man in the Emerald City."[26]

Jinjur and her army are eventually defeated by the release of an army of mice and the dispatch by Glinda the Good of another all-girl army, but a more efficient and better-equipped one. Jinjur and her troops, however, accept the victory philosophically. According to Baum (who, as a matter of fact, is reported to have been an excellent cook), "The women were so tired eating of their husbands' cooking that they all hailed the conquest of Jinjur with joy."[27] Jinjur is pardoned and returns home; in later books she appears briefly, first as a farmer's wife who bosses her husband around, and then as an energetic and generous householder who raises cream puffs, chocolate caramels, and macaroons, and is also a gifted artist.

Several other all-girl armies besides Jinjur's appear in the Oz books. The recurrence of this theme probably owes less to scorn of the military than to Baum's lifelong fascination with the theater. For many years he attempted, always without success, to turn one Oz book after the other into a musical comedy, as had been done successfully with *The Wizard of Oz*. At the time, a chorus of showgirls or chorus boys dressed as soldiers, sailors, or police was a very popular part of many such productions—as indeed it remains today: a recent Academy Awards show, for instance, featured an all-female company of dancing Canadian Mounties. *Tik-Tok of Oz* (1914) contains a comic male army consisting of sixteen officers and one private, organized by the Queen of Oogaboo, Ann Soforth. Tired of housework and of ruling over eighteen men, twenty-seven women, and forty-four children, she decides that she wants to conquer the world without hurting anyone. As might be expected, all her officers run away. Finally, *The Lost Princess of Oz* (1917) contains another all-girl army, described as "the fiercest soldiers of all. . . . They are more brave than men and they have better nerves,"[28] but this time the girl soldiers, like Baum's dreams of stage success, are only an optical illusion.

There are other touches of social satire in Baum's work, some of them, like the story of Jinjur, apparently directed more to adults than to children. In one of his non-Oz tales, *The Sea Fairies* (1911), an octopus bursts into tears when he is compared to Standard Oil. (Possibly it should be mentioned that Baum's father and other independent businessmen once tried and failed to break the stranglehold of Standard Oil on local oil production.) And in *The Patchwork Girl of Oz* an animated photograph named Victor Columbia Emerson who can clearly see into the future pursues the hero and his friends. In spite of their objections, Victor Columbia Emerson insists on playing an inane song called "My Lulu" over and over again:

> "It's the latest popular song," declared the phonograph, speaking in a sulky tone of voice. . . . "One that the feeble-minded can remember the words of and those ignorant of music can whistle or sing. That makes a popular song popular, and the time is coming when it will take the place of all other songs."[29]

Though the Oz books have always been read by children of both sexes, they have been especially popular with girls, and it's not hard to see why.[30] Oz is a world in which women and girls rule; in which they don't have to stay home and do housework, but can go exploring and have adventures. It is also, as Joel Chaston has pointed out, a world in which none of the major characters have a traditional family.[31] Instead, most of them live alone or with friends of the same sex. The Scarecrow stays with the Tin Woodman in his castle for months at a time, while

Ozma, Dorothy, Betsy, and Trot all have rooms in the palace of the Emerald City, and Glinda lives in a castle with "a hundred of the most beautiful girls of the Fairyland of Oz."[32]

The appeal of Oz seems even clearer if it is contrasted to that of contemporary books for girls. In the early years of the twentieth century, the heroes of most adventure stories were boys; girls stayed home and learned to get on better with their families. If they were rejected children like Rebecca of Sunnybrook Farm, or orphans like Anne of Green Gables and Judy in *Daddy Long-Legs*, they found or established new families. At the end of all these stories, or their sequels, the heroine grew up, fell in love, and got married.

There was of course already another famous little girl protagonist who had adventures in a magical world: Lewis Carroll's Alice. But from the point of view of most child readers (including me) her experiences were less attractive. Unlike Dorothy and Ozma, who collect loving friends and companions on their journeys, Alice travels alone, and the strange creatures she meets are usually indifferent, self-absorbed, hostile, or hectoring. Rather than helping her, as Dorothy's companions do, they make unreasonable demands: she is told to hold a screaming baby, do impossible math problems, and act as a ladies' maid. One or two of the characters seem to wish her well in a helpless way, like the White Knight, whom many readers have seen as a stand-in for Carroll himself. Moreover Wonderland, unlike Oz, turns out to be only a dream.

Most children, though they may enjoy Alice's adventures, don't want to visit Wonderland, which is full of disappearing scenery and dangerous eccentrics, some of them clearly quite insane. They prefer Oz, where life is all play and no work, and all adventures end happily.

To some extent Baum's endorsement of escapism was hidden—disguised as lighthearted comic fantasy, with a series of sweet, pretty-little-girl protagonists, the most famous of whom at first declares that all she really wants is to go home to flat, gray Kansas and see her dull, deeply depressed Uncle Henry and Aunt Em again. But, as anyone knows who has read even a few of Baum's later Oz books, Dorothy may return to Kansas after her adventures, but she doesn't stay there very long—somehow, a natural disaster (shipwreck, earthquake, whirling highways) always appears to carry her back to Oz and the magical countries that surround it. She spends more and more time there, and has more adventures. Finally, in the fifth volume of the series, Dorothy not only moves to Oz permanently, but arranges for Uncle Henry and Aunt Em (whose failing farm is about to be repossessed by the bank) to join her there. Yes, you can escape from your dreary domestic life into fairyland, Baum's books say: you can have exciting but safe adventures, make new friends, live in a castle, never have to do housework or homework, and—maybe most important of all—never grow up.

This subversive message may be one of the reasons that the Oz books took so long to become accepted as classics. For more than half a century after L. Frank Baum discovered it in 1900, the Land of Oz had a curious reputation. American children by the thousands went there happily, but authorities in the field of juvenile literature, like suspicious and conservative travel agents, refused to recommend it or even to handle tickets. Librarians would not buy the Oz books, schoolteachers would not let you write reports on them, and the best-known histories of children's books made no reference to their existence. In the 1930s and 1940s they were actually removed from many schools and libraries. As a child I had to save my allowance to buy the Oz books, because the local public library refused to carry them. This censorship was justified at the time by pointing out that the books were not beautifully written and that the characters were two-dimensional. This is arguable, but it has not prevented many other less than stylistically perfect children's books of the period from being admired and recommended. It seems more likely that in the dark years between the first and the second waves of American feminism, critics recognized the subversive power of Baum's creation.

Not until recently did the Oz books enter the canon, and in some communities they are still under attack. Fundamentalist Christians have complained that *The Wizard of Oz* contains two good witches (to them, an oxymoron) and also that, "in Oz, females assume traditional male roles, and animals are elevated to human status."[33] Apparently, if you believe in creationism, characters like the Cowardly Lion and Billina the hen, who not only talk but give good advice and help defeat evil, are a serious threat.

Yet these Ozophobes, like the Nomes, are clearly on the losing side. A new edition of Michael Patrick Hearn's exhaustive and entertaining *Annotated Wizard of Oz* has appeared; and there is now an International Wizard of Oz Club with headquarters in Kinderhook, Illinois, a name that Baum himself might have invented. In July 2000 more than four hundred fans, many of them in spectacular costume, gathered in Bloomington, Indiana, to celebrate the hundredth anniversary of Oz. They shared a five-foot-high green birthday cake in the shape of the Emerald City, and watched the current Wizard (a professor of orthodontics from San Francisco), accompanied by nine plastic pigs, take off in a giant gas balloon.

IS THERE ANYBODY THERE? WALTER DE LA MARE'S SOLITARY CHILD

Lᴵᴋᴇ many famous writers for children, Walter de la Mare had an idyllic early childhood that was cut short too soon. His first nine years were spent in a large, happy family in the outer suburbs of London, at the edge of the countryside he loved. But at ten he became a chorister and boarding student at St. Paul's Cathedral school in central London. The boys there studied and practiced and performed seven days a week, with only one hour of freedom a day. Soon memories of his early life began to fade; later he would write that "those happy, unhappy, far-away days seem like mere glimpses of a dragon-fly shimmering and darting."[1]

For the rest of his life de la Mare would try to recapture this dragonfly. He would also continue to believe that it was better to be a child than an adult. At thirty-one he wrote to a friend that growing up "is a fiasco I am more convinced every day."[2] When he was seventy-five, his biographer, Theresa Whistler (then twenty-one), "protested against this wholesale dismissal of adult life." De la Mare, who had known her since birth, insisted that

he was right. "Take your own case," he told her. "Look how di-
luted you are!"[3]

Like Wordsworth, de la Mare saw childhood as intrinsically
superior not only to adulthood but to boyhood. In 1919 he declared that

> The child divines, the boy discovers.
> The child is intuitive, inductive, the boy
>   logical, deductive.
> The child is visionary, the boy intellectual.
> The child knows that beauty is truth, the boy
>   that truth is beauty.[4]

In this sense, de la Mare remained a child all his life, preferring intuition and vision to logic and reason. In many of his
stories and poems he views the world with the intensity, innocence, and credulity of childhood. De la Mare's world, like that
of an imaginative child, is full of mystery and wonder. As he
once wrote, children do not distinguish sharply between reality
and invention: "between their dreams and their actuality looms
no impassable abyss."[5] Nature is alive; animals and insects and
birds may be conscious beings; places have strong and definite
personalities. Ghosts inhabit deserted old houses; fairies and
witches and elves haunt woods and gardens; any tree or pond
may have its attendant spirit. De la Mare's characters, especially
if they are children, are often intensely aware of these supernatural presences—sometimes, they catch a glimpse of one.

A deserted, vaguely haunted house is the subject of de la
Mare's most often anthologized poem, "The Listeners" (which I
learned by heart as a child).

> "Is there anybody there?" said the Traveller,
>   Knocking on the moonlit door;

> And his horse in the silence champed the grasses
> Of the forest's ferny floor. . . .
>
> Ay, they heard his foot upon the stirrup,
> And the sound of iron on stone,
> And how the silence surged softly backward,
> When the plunging hoofs were gone.[6]

De la Mare's sense of time often recalls that of a child. Hours, days, and seasons seem to go on forever, or telescope suddenly. Many of his characters appear to live in an eternal present, where they are shown staring so intently at some landscape, person, or creature that they are unaware of time passing. What their elders might call "daydreaming," de la Mare suggests, is in fact an intense, self-forgetful absorption in something outside the self: a condition of mind made famous by Keats, who called it "negative capability." In one story, for instance, the child Maria looks so intently at a fly on the wall that she in effect merges with it. "She seemed almost to have *become* the fly—Maria-Fly. . . . When [she] came to, it seemed she had been away for at least three centuries."[7]

There is almost always a dark side as well as a bright one to de la Mare's work. His characters are very often either lonely old people or children, and when he speaks as a child, it is usually a special kind of child: solitary, dreamy, half-frightened and half-fascinated by the world around him. One critic has even claimed that what the solitary child in de la Mare's poems and stories sees most clearly is death.[8] It is true that his work is full of unexplained disappearances, but many of them can be seen as an accurate picture of the way the world looks to many small children. Adults come and go unpredictably, and often no explanation is given, or the explanation is one that a child cannot really understand. A day or a week is much longer than it is for adults—even an hour's delay or absence may seem interminable.

Theresa Whistler's intelligent, well-researched, and wonderfully readable recent biography of de la Mare presents itself as a record of his life; but it is also a sensitive and thoughtful study of his fiction and poetry. Whistler comes to her task with important advantages: as the granddaughter of de la Mare's old friend and patron Sir Henry Newbolt, she knew him and many of his associates from infancy. As she says in her prologue, she "inherited a friendship with him already intimate through three generations."[9] She began her research for the biography shortly after de la Mare's death in 1956, when many of his friends and relatives were still alive.

Whistler does not attempt to present de la Mare as an unfairly neglected writer. If anything, she rather undervalues him. Though she claims that his work "carries the tang of authentic spiritual experience," she calls his subjects "elusive, fantastic, fine-spun and minor-keyed" and says that for her his prose is sometimes "exhausting and blood-thinning," and his "sentiment dated."[10]

But minor or dated as de la Mare may now seem even to his own biographer, he is one of the few writers of his generation who was able to discover and claim a new literary territory, and change his readers' perception of the world. Half-abandoned old houses; odd, lonely children; eccentric spinsters and bachelors; and foggy, melancholy woodlands existed before he wrote, but he described them with such intensity that it is now possible to recognize a de la Mare character, mood, or landscape anywhere.

To those who know his books, it may seem surprising that it took so long for a full-length life of de la Mare to appear. But biographers today prefer subjects who do much of the preliminary work themselves, creating themselves as dramatic public figures—something de la Mare avoided whenever possible. They also like crisis and scandal, and if possible, violence and tragedy. De la Mare's life, after his early struggles for recognition, was private and uneventful. He married at twenty-six and remained married until his wife died forty-eight years later, and he was an affectionate father to their four children. He had few enemies, and only one—unconsummated—love affair. Even his biographer calls his history "unexciting and respectable."[11]

Essentially de la Mare had the life that Forster's Leonard Bast, the doomed clerk of *Howard's End*, might have had with better luck. Like Leonard Best, he began in the lowest strata of the middle class: his father died in 1877 when he was four, plunging de la Mare's mother and her seven children into poverty. As a choirboy at St. Paul's Cathedral between the ages of ten and sixteen he received a good education. But when his voice changed, he had to leave school. There was no money to send him to a university; instead he became a low-ranking clerk in the city, overworked and underpaid. The same thing happened to Kenneth Grahame, the author of *The Wind in the Willows*, and with some of the same effect, though he was luckier in finding a less demanding job with the Bank of England—and like de la Mare, Grahame accepted adulthood only reluctantly.

For eighteen years de la Mare worked fifty-seven hours a week in the statistical department of the Anglo-American Oil Company, adding columns of figures and copying documents. Hating this organization, which he once described as "carnivorous,"[12] he lived as much as he could in the world of his imagination, believing in the existence of what he called "another reality," which would be sought through "make-believe, daydream, empathy, [and] free association."[13]

According to all accounts de la Mare was a good-looking, sensitive, romantic young man, with vague but intense intellectual and literary ambitions. Like Forster's Leonard Bast, he married unwisely, and probably under pressure—in his case, two and a half months before the birth of his first child. His wife, Elfie, was eleven years older, a clerk in an insurance office, and the leading lady of the local South London dramatic society. She was essentially uneducated and rather silly, but from the beginning she believed wholly in de la Mare as a writer, and for many years, starting even before the marriage, she took on the task of sending out his manuscripts in order to spare him the pain of rejection slips.

De la Mare was also lucky in that his ambitions were more focused than those of Leonard Bast: from the age of twenty he was determined to be an author. Often, after office hours ended at six thirty, he remained at his desk until midnight in order to write. Presently this industry was rewarded: his first story was accepted when he was only twenty-two, though he didn't publish a book until seven years later. He was fortunate also in that he was not taken up by well-meaning but ultimately destructive well-to-do people like Forster's Schlegels. Instead he gradually became friends with other young writers, including Rupert Brooke, W. H. Davies, Ralph Hodgson, and Edward Thomas.

Unlike most male writers of his time (or ours) de la Mare enjoyed domesticity. He was good at housekeeping: he could change diapers and bake a cake. But overwork and constant worry about money dragged him down. In his twenties and early thirties he was often depressed and troubled by doubts about his own ability as a writer. By the time he was thirty-five he had published several books of poetry and the fantasy novel *Henry Brocken*, but though reviews were good, he was still earning almost nothing from his writing, and only £143 a year from Anglo-American Oil.

Now, however, his luck improved. His friend Henry Newbolt (who at the time was a far better known poet than de la Mare) managed to get him a government grant of two hundred pounds a year, and persuaded him to quit his job and accept it. Suddenly de la Mare had time to write. Poems and stories and essays poured forth; he began to review regularly and started a juvenile fantasy based on the tales he had told his four children, *The Three Mulla-Mulgars*, which is generally recognized as one of the sources of Tolkien's *The Hobbit*. From then on de la Mare still had periods of self-doubt and depression, but essentially he was out of the woods—though in his case this seems the wrong metaphor, since nothing delighted and fascinated him more than an ancient and shadowy forest.

The landscape of de la Mare's stories and poems, of course, was not unique to him, but part of the late-nineteenth-century Romantic tradition of the haunted English countryside: the numinous, isolated woods and fields and marshes that provided the background for writers like Arthur Machen, Forrest Reid, Lord Dunsany, and Sylvia Townsend Warner. Their best-known stories are set by preference in a rural world that was vanishing in their lifetimes, a world not yet shrunken by the telephone and the motorcar. Its characteristic atmosphere of romantic melancholy is a sort of pathetic fallacy—loss of landscape embodied in landscape. What makes de la Mare's writing exceptional is that for him this scenery and the mixture of sadness and enchantment it embodied were often the central subject of his work: foreground as well as background.

Though the landscape that most moved de la Mare was that of southwest England, especially Devon and Cornwall, his ancestry was in fact part Scotch and part French Huguenot. A geneticist might suggest that this inheritance made him both a dreamer and a Puritan—a combination that might help to explain his current loss of popularity. Today, passion is expected to express itself in physical data: size and color of parts, number of orgasms, type of contraception used; the description of a love affair that doesn't include such details seems fuzzy and incomplete. But though de la Mare could be deeply romantic, the erotic is almost wholly absent from his work. According to his biographer, Theresa Whistler, he was not much interested in sex. He was, as she puts it, "romantic, fastidious, and private," someone for whom "the physical aspects of *anything*, not merely of love, would always be secondary."[14]

When he was thirty-eight, and just beginning to be well known, de la Mare fell in love with the literary editor of a magazine to which he was a contributor, the *Saturday Westminster Review*. Naomi Royde-Smith was thirty-three—a lively, intelligent, and independent woman with a romantic imagination. She had always wanted to be the soul mate and muse of a great writer, and de la Mare was happy to assign her that role.

For the next three years Naomi and de la Mare were intensely in love with each other. But, evidently to her annoyance, the affair remained platonic, though he wrote her nearly eight hundred love letters. Even so he was often tormented by guilt; as he once wrote to her, "Surely a man with a wife and four children has no justification for allowing *any* of his flock of selves to stray from the domestic fold."[15] Also, according to his biographer, in some ways he preferred the idea of Naomi to the reality.

> I long to get things over, to have them safe in memory [he wrote to her]. . . . Even you are almost best in memory, where I cannot change you, nor you yourself.[16]

In the summer of 1913 de la Mare spent three days in Naomi's room, but apparently refused to sleep with her. From then on, though the letters continued, Naomi became increasingly impatient with his demands on her time and attention, and the relationship went downhill fast.

*

Soon after the start of World War I de la Mare contracted appendicitis, followed by complications that kept him convalescent for many months. Another man might have resented the enforced inactivity and separation from historic events, but de la Mare, who had had to share his mother with six other children and his wife with four, enjoyed being fed and cosseted by nurses. His return home brought on a period of depression, but in 1915 he had two strokes of good luck. First, he was made a Royal Society of Literature professor (a largely honorary office) and granted a pension of one hundred pounds. Then Rupert Brooke died in Greece and left everything to three friends and poets, of whom de la Mare was one. Death transformed Brooke into a world-class hero and best-selling poet, and the resulting royalties gave de la Mare economic security for the rest of his life.

In 1921 de la Mare published his strangest and most famous work of fiction, *The Memoirs of a Midget*. It is a tour de force: a middle-aged man's fully imagined and convincing vision of what it would be like to be a young woman between two and three feet tall (de la Mare never gives his heroine's exact height). His narrator, Miss M—whose full name we never learn—is, like her creator, self-educated, thoughtful, dreamy, and fascinated by natural phenomena from the stars to the patterns of lichen. She begins life as a sheltered only child, becomes an orphan, falls in love with a beautiful and ambitious full-sized woman, and is courted by a male dwarf. Later she is taken up by London society as a kind of pet, and finally she joins a circus.

According to Theresa Whistler, de la Mare always spoke of Miss M as a real person, a kind of imaginary companion. He saw himself as equally isolated and peculiar; and Whistler is surely right in tracing a connection between Miss M's emotional life

and de la Mare's. Like her, de la Mare felt an alternating pleasure
and distaste when he was lionized by London society hostesses;
like her, he both enjoyed and resented being taken care of.

Though Theresa Whistler does not point this out, it is also
possible to see echoes of his relationship with Naomi Royde-
Smith in the story. When Miss M tells the dwarf who loves her,
"I share my secretest thoughts—my imagination, with you; isn't
that a kind of love?"[17] it is easy to imagine de la Mare giving the
same excuse to Naomi. And when Fanny, the young woman
Miss M romantically adores, complains of Miss M's rejection of
physical contact, we may hear Naomi's voice accusing de la Mare.

> "You said you loved me—oh yes. But touch me, come here"—
> she laid her hand almost fondly on her breast—"and be hu-
> manly generous, no. That's no more your nature than—than
> a changeling's. Contamination, perhaps!"[18]

Like most good novels *The Memoirs of a Midget* can be read in
many ways. It can be seen as an inversion of de la Mare's psychological situation: Miss M is an adult in a child's body, while de la
Mare is in some ways a child in an adult's body. It also works as
an allegory about the position of middle-class women in the late
nineteenth century: petted and minimized when weak, condemned
when they want independence. Except for the days when she is
displaying herself in the circus, Miss M never earns a shilling;
people take care of her because she is helpless and cute. Only after great difficulties is she able to live alone, on inherited money.

Miss M's friend Fanny, on the other hand, has to earn her living as a teacher; at one point she comes to Miss M desperate to
borrow money (probably for an abortion, though de la Mare
does not spell this out). Hard as she tries, Fanny cannot survive
on her own. She ends up making a loveless marriage and blam-
ing all her troubles on Miss M, whom she accuses of having
been her enemy for years. In terms of the story this accusation

is cruel and unreasonable, but it works symbolically. Rich, child-ish, dependent Victorian women were in a sense the enemies of poor working girls like Fanny. If the author of *The Memoirs of a Midget* had been a woman, the book might now be acclaimed as an early feminist classic.

Classic or not, it is impressively well written. De la Mare cared about prose, and his is often brilliant; no one can set a mood or describe landscape and weather better:

Soon after six . . . a storm, which all the afternoon had been steadily piling its leaden vapours into space, began to break. . . . The very air seemed to thicken, and every tree stood up as if carved out of metal. Of a sudden a great wind, with heavy plashing drops of rain, swept roaring round the house, thick with dust and green leaves torn from the disheveled summer trees. There was a hush. The darkness intensified, and then a vast sheet of lightning seemed to picture all Kent in my eyes, and the air was full of water.[19]

The emotional intensity and subtle, haunting charm of *The Memoirs of a Midget* also power de la Mare's best stories. As his biographer points out, very often they are told from the viewpoint of a child coolly observing the passions and tragedies of adults, or by an uninvolved narrator to whom strangers confide odd or dreadful histories. Many of them recall the ghost stories of Henry James, whom de la Mare admired. A few of these tales, such as "Seaton's Aunt," "Crewe," and "Miss Duveen," are still occasionally anthologized; they deserve to be classics, and so does de la Mare's early, haunting tale "The Riddle," in which seven children, singly or in pairs, vanish into an old oak chest in a house deep in the country—perhaps into death, perhaps only into adulthood.

*

Time, which de la Mare so often portrayed as flexible, in the end was ruthless to him. Taste in literature, like taste in food, changes. The complex, sugary custards and meringues and soufflés that crowned a company dinner fifty or a hundred years ago are seldom seen today—like many of the writers most admired in the early twentieth century.

De la Mare's work, once celebrated on both sides of the Atlantic, is now little known here. Almost none of his many books are still in print, and his brilliant anthology of "poems for children of all ages," *Come Hither*, is only available in secondhand bookshops. Like old-fashioned desserts, much of his work now seems overelaborate, too full of air and sugar.

Though de la Mare was long considered a master of ghostly fantasy, his spooky tales may be too low-key for current tastes. In his time readers—at least middle-class readers—were somewhat sheltered from the violence of the world; it did not take much to create a pleasing shudder. Now many authors feel they must compete with the horrors served on television; as a result popular fantasy fiction is crowded with exploding bodies, drooling vampires, carnivorous reptiles, and repellently decaying corpses raised from the grave. To readers used to such coarse fare, de la Mare's skillful, haunting tales and verses may seem "bloodless"—which they usually literally are.

In another sense, however, many of de la Mare's stories are as strange and terrible as any told today—and often far better written. In contemporary thrillers evil usually assaults the central character from without; he may be terrified, injured, or even killed, but he is usually sympathetic. But in some of de la Mare's most successful tales ordinary-looking heroes, very like his readers, turn out to have dark histories and violent impulses. Often, simply being alone or idle is enough to call them up. As the heroine of "The Wharf" says, "If you remain empty, ideas come creeping in. . . . It is always dangerous—leaving doors ajar."[20]

Occasionally, evil in de la Mare is external; but if so, it tends to be embodied not in obvious villains, but in people and places that at first sight seem familiar or even reassuring: a spinster aunt who sends generous food parcels to her nephew at boarding school; a picturesque old cathedral in the depths of the country. Only gradually do we realize that Seaton's aunt, in the story of that name, has psychologically devoured her nephew, or that the country cathedral has been taken over by demons.

De la Mare's collections of fairy tales for children, *Broomsticks* and *The Lord Fish*, are well worth rereading. Nothing is harder than to invent a convincing modern fairy story, but in a couple of cases de la Mare manages it, notably in "The Lovely Mywfawny," which features a father who, like de la Mare himself at one point, cannot bear the idea that his daughter will marry and leave home. The story was written the summer that Florence de la Mare announced her engagement to a family friend—upon which her father "blurted out 'I am sorry to hear it.'"[21] Yet his sense of humor and proportion reasserted itself, and in the tale the foolishly jealous father is turned into an ass.

It is harder to make a case for de la Mare's verse. In his own lifetime he was even more famous as a poet than as a storyteller, but today much of his work seems dated. His contemporary Middletown Murray called it a "flourish of clichés,"[22] and it is weakened further by de la Mare's conviction that only certain subjects, certain emotions, and a certain diction are truly "poetic." From the beginning he thought that his "other reality" should be described in a language different from that of everyday life: it demanded fine writing and a special vocabulary.

De la Mare's verses are full of inversions, of words already archaic at the time (*'tis, aught, eve, amidst*), and of capitalized nouns (Fate and Evening). He prefers the standard late Romantic subjects: nature, the fleetingness of beauty, children, minor supernatural figures, and lost love. The subject for which he became most famous was the mysteriousness of empty landscapes and deserted or half-deserted buildings. And in spite of their old-fashioned diction, some of his verses on these subjects still convey a subtle thrill.

Though I loved many of de la Mare's poems as a child, I found others disturbing. I was especially troubled by the fish in the frying pan that "put up his mouth / And moaned 'Alas!' "[23] and by Poor Jim Jay who "Got stuck fast / In Yesterday"[24] and then slowly vanished. It did not occur to me, of course, that de la Mare might have been foreseeing his own fate. But by the time "Poor Jim Jay" appeared there were already signs that the kind of verse he wrote was being replaced by the work of writers like T. S. Eliot and Ezra Pound. His children's poems were still anthologized, but critics began to see him as stuck in Yesterday; and after his death he gradually began to vanish from literary history.

Probably many writers, if given the choice, would prefer to be successful and honored in their own lifetimes rather than after death. De la Mare, in spite of his air of dreamy estrangement from the contemporary world, now seems very much a figure of his time, and I was not surprised to learn that he disliked most mid-twentieth-century writing and voted Tory.

The last years of his life followed the standard pattern of literary success. He continued to write and publish, and to gather awards and honors—though he twice refused the knighthood that he had already covertly awarded himself by creating the benevolent and learned Sir Walter of *Memoirs of a Midget*. He had lengthening periods of poor health; but for him this had advantages. Being taken care of by others, he once said, brought him "a curious inward happiness,"[25] and he liked the dreams that morphine gave him. He was horrified by news of the atomic bomb and concentration camps, but continued to enjoy the things that had always made him happiest: reading, nature, his children, and the companionship of other writers.

De la Mare died at eighty-three, surrounded by friends and family, and devotedly cared for by a young nurse. And though his reputation did not long survive him, he escaped the pathetic fate he had ironically predicted for himself in one of his best stories, "Willows." Here, a once-promising poet turns out not to have died young and romantically, but to have survived as "a tubby little man" with "bright blue eyes of an extraordinary intensity"[26] whose world has become obscure and incomprehensible. (De la Mare was also rather small, with bright blue eyes, and by the time the story appeared in 1929, he had become rather stout.)

But his waning popularity and unsensational life also saved de la Mare from what, in the same story, a character calls "the danger worse than death" of predatory biographers and critics, "these so-called 'lovers' of poetry—these parasites—their jealousies, their quarrels, the pretences, their petty curiosity, their suffocating silliness."[27] Instead he had to wait nearly forty years for a serious biography; but in Theresa Whistler he found one without any of these failings. Her perceptive and thoughtful book was worth the wait.

JOHN MASEFIELD'S
BOXES OF DELIGHT

I must down to the seas again," declares the first stanza of "Sea Fever," John Masefield's best-known poem:

> To the lonely sea and the sky,
> And all I ask is a tail ship and a star to steer her by.[1]

But Masefield did not go down to the seas again. In fact, this "poet of the sea" suffered from seasickness, and at the age of seventeen he left the merchant marine, which had inspired his most famous work, and spent the rest of his life well inland. As soon as he could afford it, he moved with his wife and children to an increasingly grand series of English country houses where, for the rest of his life, he enjoyed the quiet existence of a rural squire.

The private Masefield was the opposite of the Masefield projected in his books: the tough, hearty, gregarious old sea dog, full of yarns and tales of adventure in foreign lands or on the ocean among rough men in bad weather (or among bad men in rough weather). In reality he was gentle, courtly, self-effacing, literary, and fond of children and nature.[2] His best writing, according to many critics, was in his books for children: the adventure stories *Martin Hyde* and *Jim Davis*, and the brilliant fantasies, *The Midnight Folk* and *The Box of Delights*.

Modern writers, even poets—who might have been sympathetic, since some of them have equally incongruous public and private lives—have been dismissive of Masefield, or have sought him out mainly because of his connection to other writers. The gifted poet and critic Daniel Hoffman, for instance, visited Masefield in 1961 in order to ask him about Yeats, whom he had known as a young man. Though he appreciated some aspects of Masefield's poetry, its "moments of fierce archaic emotion" and "clear and supple verse,"[3] the visit was disappointing. When Hoffman arrived in a steady drizzle at what he descibes as "a large, ungainly mock-Tudor structure in brown stucco with a dark roof,"[4] Masefield's daughter, Judith, mistook him for the television repairman. His interview took place in a "vestibule" lit by one bare hanging lightbulb; afterward he was served tea and a "sticky sweet cake."[5]

Perhaps as a result of this unhappy experience, Hoffman afterward characterized Masefield's daughter as "a squarely built middle-aged woman in . . . groundgripper shoes"[6] and Masefield himself as "an anachronism who embodied very parochial British values" and whose "ambitious narratives are hobbled by conventionality."[7]

It is true that Masefield's poems today may seem dated, encumbered by a conventional adherence to meter and rhyme, and by his determination to tell stories in verse. A case can probably still be made for works like *Reynard the Fox*, and Muriel Spark, in her brilliant early study of Masefield's work, has done her best to make it[8]—but not all readers have been convinced. In many ways it is appropriate that Masefield should end up most famous as a writer for children. For one thing, he had the history that seems to be characteristic for authors of juvenile classics. In a sense some part of him did not leave childhood slowly and naturally, but was abruptly forced underground, where it was preserved unchanged. As a result, in his writing he was always able to think and feel as a child.

Masefield's daughter, Judith, in a brief memoir, describes her father as a wonderful playmate—essentially, another child. Once, when she was housebound with a sprained ankle, he bought her a toy butcher's shop; and she reports that "we played tirelessly until my foot was well, taking it in turn to be butcher and customers."[9] Judith also notes that in old age, "When asked to name two great books of modern times, he said without hesitation, *The Wind in the Willows* by Kenneth Grahame and *The Tailor of Gloucester* by Beatrix Potter."[10]

Although he wrote a short literary autobiography, *So Long to Learn*, in 1952, Masefield was always secretive and vague about his early years, except with a few close friends. He did not want his biography to be written or his letters published—indeed, according to rumor, he put a curse on anyone who might attempt this. It was not until 1978, more than eleven years after his death, that the first biography, by Constance Babington-Smith, appeared. (Apparently the curse was ineffective, for Babington-Smith went on to publish several more books.)

It now seems ironic that Masefield should have tried to suppress the most interesting aspects of his life. The truth, when it finally emerged, was far more remarkable and also more impressive than the conventional picture of an easy and confident rise to respectability and literary eminence. Indeed, when a reader knows what obstacles Masefield had to overcome, and how hard he worked for his success, it is hard not to feel amazement and admiration.

According to Masefield, until he was six he was "living in Paradise."[11] Paradise was located in Ledbury, Hertfordshire, where Masefield was born in June 1878, the third of five children of a local solicitor. But in January 1895 his mother died after giving birth to her sixth child. Earlier writers reported that his father also died soon afterward. In fact, Mr. Masefield senior survived for more than six years, during which he became increasingly disturbed mentally; he ended his life in a local hospital. Meanwhile, care of Masefield and his brothers and sisters passed to a dim, silent uncle, an unsympathetic aunt, and a critical and suspicious governess whom all the children detested.

Masefield was a solitary, sensitive, dreamy boy, who loved wandering in the countryside and telling himself long stories. Before his mother's death his relationship to nature had been idyllic and Wordsworthian.

All that I looked upon was beautiful, and known by me to be beautiful, but also known by me to be, as it were, only the shadow of something much more beautiful.[12]

Now everything began to go wrong: he lost "the ecstatic bliss of my earliest childhood." "Certain . . . sorrows then crushed my power to enter it: and for a long time I mourned, thinking that I had been damned, as some of my elders had said I should be. The effect upon myself could not be distinguished from damnation."[13] Masefield's aunt believed that books and the arts were a waste of time, "and worse still they opened the door to an immoral life."[14] When Masefield said that he would like to study art or literature, she was scornful. "It was agreed that I had no talent" and "was always far too much given to idle reading."[15] Instead, he was literally shipped off, at thirteen, to a merchant marine training ship in Liverpool, the *Conway*.

It is hard to imagine a teenager less suited to the merchant marine than this shy, nervous, unhappy boy. At first he was mercilessly bullied, and had to fight off unwelcome homosexual attentions. But presently he was befriended by an older student who became his hero. Masefield's attachment to this boy, whom he referred to later only as H. B., was deep and long-lasting, and when H. B. shipped out, Masefield's misery was intense. "Nothing in my boyhood hurt me so cruelly," he wrote later. "I have thought of him every day for more than half a century."[16]

After a while Masefield adjusted to life on the training ship, though his fellow students, when interviewed later in the days of his fame, remembered him as an "odd fish," who didn't mix with the others, but spent all his spare time reading.[17] His first ocean voyage after graduation was traumatic. Now sixteen, he was excited and moved by the beauty of the sea and by the bravery and endurance of the sailors. But he was also violently seasick, worn down by the heavy work, and stunned by the brutality and nonstop blasphemy of life on board. The passage around Cape Horn was too much for him. By the time his ship reached Chile, he was ill with a combination of sunstroke, exhaustion, and nerves, and was invalided home to England.

Masefield wanted to try another career, preferably as a painter or writer, but as soon as he had recovered, his aunt insisted that he go back to sea. He was sent to New York to join another ship; but when he arrived, he failed to report for duty. Detectives were sent after him, but without success. Like many other rebellious adolescents, he had disappeared into the underworld. With a drinking companion whom he later called "a disreputable ruffian,"[18] he traveled around the United States as a hobo, begging, hitching rides on trains, sleeping rough, and occasionally taking odd jobs.

Eventually Masefield resurfaced in New York, where for two months he worked sixteen hours a day in a saloon, and then for two years in a carpet factory in Yonkers, just outside the city. He lived in a local boardinghouse and spent most of his disposable income on cheap editions of the English classics.

But he was now determined to become a writer, and in 1897, at nineteen, he managed to get back to London. There he earned his keep first as a clerk in a bank, an occupation of which he appears to have been greatly ashamed, and then as a hack journalist. Gradually he began to publish verse and stories. In 1902, when he was twenty-four, his first book of poems appeared, and ten years later he was a recognized poet and novelist.

Established authors who occasionally turn to writing for children often reveal far more of themselves than they do in their adult prose or poetry. For one thing, they are as it were on vacation, and under no pressure to produce a Great Work. Masefield was sensitive to criticism, and modest about his literary abilities. He knew from the start that he would never be as good a writer as his friends Yeats and Synge. What he was, he sometimes said, was a storyteller, and in his children's books, all he needed to do was tell a good story. As a result, his tone there is easier and more relaxed; there is no sense of critics breathing down his neck as he writes.

For Masefield there was another advantage to juvenile fiction. He had always been uneasy about his lack of formal education: unlike most of his friends and colleagues, he had not been lucky enough to go to university. Instead, he had left school at twelve. But now he was writing for an audience that had no more education than he did. It was not only unnecessary to display erudition, it was counterproductive.

In his children's books Masefield also seems to feel no need to present a hero who embodies or develops the standard British male virtues. For his boy protagonists the split between child and adult, between private and public self, has not yet occurred. They can be reckless, frightened, disobedient, they can make mistakes and even weep, for after all they are only children.

*

The authors who write most successfully for children write not as an adult talking (sometimes talking down) to a juvenile audience, but as the child in themselves. Masefield was able to enter into the fantasies of childhood and respond to the natural world with a child's wonder and enthusiasm, because he was, in some ways, still a boy.

Masefield's first works for children, *A Book of Discoveries* and *Martin Hyde*, appeared in 1910, the year his son, Lewis, was born, and when his daughter, Judith, was five years old. *A Book of Discoveries*, though presented as a story, is really a series of informal lectures on local history and ecology, possibly suggested by the family's recent move from London to a house in Buckinghamshire. It describes the explorations of two rather undifferentiated English boys under the guidance of a neighbor, Mr. Hampden, a thinly disguised version of the author. Mr. Hampden knows everything about the countryside, with an emphasis on the battles that were fought there from Roman times onward. He teaches the boys how to rig a model schooner, chart the local river, predict the weather, build a camp, practice amateur archaeology, and understand the habits of birds, beasts, and fish.

A Book of Discoveries strongly recalls an earlier Canadian children's classic, *Two Little Savages* (1903) by Ernest Thompson Seton, which was designed to teach Indian woodcraft to boys. But perhaps because the English landscape is so much tamer, or because the characters and plot are less developed, Masefield's book never had as great a success, and today it is very slow going. Most of it was clearly written by the public, adult Masefield.

Martin Hyde, or The Duke's Messenger, is a much better and more original book, an exciting adventure story set in the late seventeenth century, full of spies, disguises, midnight rides, battles, imprisonment, and escape. It also, most unusually, contains a heroine who does more than allow herself to be rescued. In Masefield's adult work the female characters tend to be unde-veloped; often they are peripheral to the plot or totally absent. As G. Wilson Knight puts it,

> Ships, often regarded as living creatures, have the grace and beauty men usually attribute to women, whose place they fill in Masefield's narratives.[19]

But Amelia Carew is a convincing character: a beautiful and brave teenager, and a very active and successful spy. She is also several years older than Martin Hyde, to whom she relates as to a younger brother. She represents the type of woman Masefield was most drawn to: strong, competent, and mature. Constance, his wife, was eleven years his senior, and he had several ro-mantic but probably unconsummated love affairs with women who were older than he.

To give a character the name of Hyde, especially at the time, was to suggest a connection with Stevenson's masterpiece; and Martin Hyde can be seen in some ways as the hidden rebellious adolescent self of his respectable author. The book is told in the first person, and Martin says on the first page, "I know not the day of my birth"[20]—a claim that Masefield often made himself. (The suggestion of a mysterious origin was false, since the date—June 1, 1878—was written in local records.) Like Masefield, Mar-tin Hyde has an idyllic early life, which ends abruptly when he is orphaned at twelve and sent to live with an unsympathetic un-cle. He portrays himself as a semi-juvenile delinquent: disobedi-ent, sneaky, impulsive, alternately frightened and foolhardy. Shortly after the book begins he breaks into a neighbor's house, where he overhears a plot against the monarchy. He is discov-ered by the conspirators, and becomes half-reluctantly attached to a bad and failing cause: the ill-starred Monmouth Rebellion, which attempted to overthrow the government of James II and put the Duke of Monmouth on the English throne.

Very soon Martin Hyde finds himself at sea. The indignities he suffers cause him to remark that "for brutal, thoughtless injustice, it is difficult to beat the merchant ship."[21] Like Masefield at the same age, he is at first "much ashamed at having to work as a common ship's boy."[22] But he learns from the experience, and comes to respect the sailors, realizing that, in his words, "It is nothing to be proud of that your parents are rich enough to keep your hands clean of joyless, killing toil, at an age when many better men are old in slavery."[23]

Later, in a striking departure from the traditions of popular boys' fiction, Martin Hyde warns his young readers against "the life of adventure":

It is a life of sordid unquiet, pursued without plan, like the life of an animal. Have you seen a dog trying to cross a busy street? There is the adventurer. Or the rabbit on the cliff, in his state of continual panic; he, too, lives the adventurous life.[24]

Most atypically for an adventure story of the period, *Martin Hyde* refuses to glorify war. When the duke's forces go "foraging," Martin remarks:

It was theft with violence, coloured over by some little touch of law. . . . We were like an army of locusts, eating up everything as we passed.[25]

The battles are scenes of terror and confusion, in which Martin Hyde, unlike most boy heroes, does not rise to the occasion:

Another ball came just over my head, with a scream which made my heart quite sick. I sat down cowering under a ruined thorn-tree by the road, crying like a little child. . . . I saw a man staggering down the road towards me, holding his side with both hands. He fell into the road, dead, not far from me. Then others came past . . . in a long horrible procession, men without weapons, without hands, shot in the head, in the body, lacerated, bleeding, limping. . . . It was nothing but a time of pain, a roaring, booming horror with shrieks in it.[26]

Martin Hyde is no longer in print in England or America; perhaps it is too downbeat to survive as juvenile fiction; but as a first-rate, morally serious historical novel it can sustain comparison with Stevenson, whom Masefield much admired; it should be better known.

Jim Davis, which appeared the following year, in 1911, is much shorter, and also less ambitious and dark; perhaps this is why it has remained in print. It is the story of a boy who falls in with smugglers on the coast of Devon in 1812. The book is full of incident: there are gypsies, mysterious night riders, a sea voyage, storms, caves, fights, pursuits, and of course a sunken treasure. The influence of *Treasure Island* is also apparent in the figure of the gypsy Marah, who is a kind of ambiguous substitute father for Jim and his friend Hugh. Like Mr. Hampden in *A Book of Discoveries*, he teaches the boys the rudiments of rigging and sailing ships, and other kinds of practical expertise. But Marah, like Long John Silver in *Treasure Island*, turns out to be a criminal—one of the gang of smugglers. Unlike Long John, however, he reforms at the end of the book and becomes a respectable landsman. Also, though Jim is imprisoned by the smugglers when he is caught spying on them, he does not witness or take part in their crimes. In *Treasure Island*, on the other hand, Jim Hawkins not only sees men die, he kills one of the pirates himself—though in self-defense.

In *Jim Davis* Masefield not only tells an exciting story, he writes vividly and even poetically about physical activity and the natural world. Though it was now fifteen years since he had been to sea, his memory remained clear. When the smuggling ship lies off the coast of Devon at night, Jim says:

> . . . it was so still, so very peaceful, that we could hear the waves breaking on the beach with a noise of hushing and of slipping shingle, as each wave passed with a hiss to slither back in a rush of foam broken by tiny stones.[27]

Jim Davis, like *Martin Hyde*, draws in many other ways on Masefield's own early experience. Like Masefield, Jim is an orphan sent to live with unpleasant relatives. "My aunt and uncle had no children of their own, and no great fondness for the children of others,"[28] he tells the reader, something that might well be said of Masefield's own aunt and uncle. Like Masefield, at ten he is sent away to school, which at first he detests. But Jim's life turns out happier than his author's; Masefield provides him with an ideal substitute mother as well as a substitute father: the kind and devoted housekeeper Mrs. Cottier, whom he rescues in a storm.

The Midnight Folk, which first appeared in 1927, is a wonderful, very inventive fantasy for younger children. It appears to be partly set in Masefield's childhood home and in Masefield's own childhood in the 1880s. Travel is by horse, carriage, or broomstick, and the young hero's friend Ellen, the housemaid, speaks of "my grandfather's time, in the French wars."[29]

The plot centers around Kay Harker's search for two lost treasures: one from a pirate ship, the other the spoils of a highwayman's robberies. In his quest Kay is aided by several animals and by his own forgotten toys, which are lovingly listed and described. On the other side is Kay's unpleasant governess, whom he later admitted was based on the one he hated as a boy. He is also opposed by a coven of witches and two sly and treacherous cats. The forces of evil turn out to be led by a sinister wizard called Abner Brown, who I am sorry to say is an American. Abner's attitude toward the English landscape is one that Masefield, who had ambiguous feelings about Americans, was familiar with. "I fell right plumb in love with this green countryside, so full of real old buildings,"[30] Abner says, and he can hardly wait to buy some land and start digging it up.

The Midnight Folk has the air of having been created episode by episode, without much advance planning—in the manner of a story told night after night to a child. All kinds of extraneous events and characters keep appearing, as if a child had requested them. The reader can almost hear him or her saying: "Put in some Indians, please. Put in some mermaids. And flying, and a desert island." This method of storytelling can be successful, as many parents have found—but it can also somewhat overwhelm a narrative. James Barrie, in *Peter Pan*, followed a similar method: he used the stories he had told the Davies boys and the games he had played with them on holiday. The play that grew out of these stories and games also includes Indians, mermaids, pirates, and flying, all held together by Barrie's genius. *The Midnight Folk* is even more diverse. Kay not only flies, and encounters Indians, mermaids, and pirates, he also travels in time and space, goes to sea on a model sailing ship manned by mice, and sees King Arthur and his knights.

Moreover, with remarkable inventiveness, Masefield introduces several incidents and characters that prefigure, and possibly lie behind, those in later children's classics. At one point, for instance, Kay Harker becomes a bat and flies through the night under the guidance of another bat; later, with the help of an otter, he becomes an otter—just as T. H. White's boy King Arthur does in *The Sword in the Stone*, published eleven years later. Kay also meets a greedy, selfish lowlife character called Rat, who appears to be the direct ancestor of Templeton in E. B.

White's *Charlottes's Web*. Like Templeton, he saves the day—but only for a price, which must be paid in half-spoiled food.

The Midnight Folk is perhaps most remarkable for the way in which it evokes a child's consciousness. Kay, who seems to be about eight or nine years old, still does not clearly distinguish among reality, dreams, and imagination. When he is bored in the schoolroom, he diverts himself by playing games under the table:

> When he had scraped off a slipper, he could push it about
> with his toes, and imagine that it was a canoe full of Redskins
> on the warpath, going down the rapids; or a diving bell . . .
> bringing up treasure from one of the ships of the Armada; or
> great-grandpa Harker's ship, the *Plunderer*, engaging seven
> French privateers . . .[31]

Kay moves easily and naturally from fantasy to reality, and both are deeply satisfying to him, just as they were to Masefield as a small child. Like Masefield, he imagines tigers under his bed at night, and the figures of his daily life easily enter his fantasies. His governess becomes a witch, and the angry gamekeeper on the neighboring estate a wizard; his favorite cat and his lost toys are loyal and heroic companions. And though Kay does not get to keep the treasure, at the end of the book he finds something better: a kind and affectionate guardian, Caroline Louisa, who sends his governess away.

Eight years later, in 1935, Masefield published his most popular children's book, *The Box of Delights, or When the Wolves Were Running*. It is a sequel to *The Midnight Folk*, and has the same hero, Kay Harker. However, though Kay is only a year older, the story has leapt forward in time half a century. We are now in a world that includes telephones, automobiles, and airplanes, and feisty litle girls who refuse to play the feminine role. *The Box of Delights* takes place during the Christmas holidays,

when Kay is home from school for the first time, along with
Jemima, Susan, Maria, and Peter Jones. In *The Midnight Folk*
these were the names of his forgotten toys; now they are real
children, staying with Kay and Caroline Louisa while their parents are abroad.

The witch governess Sylvia Daisy Pouncer and the wizard
Abner Brown are still around, and now they are married. Abner
Brown is the head of a gang of jewel thieves, but he also dab-
bles in magic. He has disguised himself and his gang as members of a theological college; on occasion, they transform
themselves into wolves. They already control many magical devices, including a fleet of taxis that can become airplanes and
kidnap unsuspecting passengers. Abner is after the Box of Delights, which has magic powers. Currently it belongs to an old
puppeteer called Cole Hawlings, who, when hard-pressed by
the gang, gives the box to Kay.

The plot of the book is largely powered by Abner's attempts
to find the box, in the course of which he and his gang kidnap
Cole Hawlings, two of Kay's friends, his guardian, Caroline
Louisa, and the entire staff of the local cathedral, including the
bishop and the choir. If they cannot be rescued, there will be no
midnight service on Christmas Eve. The climax of the story thus
involves a full-scale conflict between good and evil, along with
a record-breaking snowstorm.

Who is the mysterious old puppeteer Cole Hawlings, and
what is his Box of Delights, which gives one the power to travel
in time and space? He appeared first, as critics have noted, in
Masefield's long narrative poem *King Cole* (1923), where he re-
vived a failing traveling circus and brought joy and inspiration to
an entire town. From the point of view of a folklorist, Cole is the
"magic helper," or, in Jungian terms, the guide or sage whom the
hero meets at the beginning of his quest. In the poem he is a
ragged old man who plays the flute and is followed by birds,
beasts, and butterflies: both a benevolent version of the Pied

Piper and a pagan nature god or Green Man. He also recalls John Masefield, who had a deep love of animals and birds; his daughter later wrote, "I often saw him cross the lawn with a mob of birds following, for his pocket was always filled with crumbs."[32] Cole Hawlings in *The Box of Delights* can summon butterflies, birds, and beasts with his panpipes, and turn a room into a forest. But he cannot protect himself or his box from Abner Brown; he needs the help of Kay and the other children.

In the real world, at this time, Masefield was fifty-seven and at the height of his fame, but he was also beset with public duties and demands. In 1930 he had been named poet laureate, and though he had once promised that he would not write to order, he now continually provided verses for ceremonial occasions. He was constantly asked to write, to speak, to answer letters, to travel abroad, and to appear at public events. It would not be surprising if, like Cole Hawlings, Masefield felt himself surrounded and even imprisoned. Moreover, outside his country retreat, in the larger world, things were not going well. In 1935, all over Europe, the wolves were running.

And what of the Box of Delights, which the old magician can no longer guard and must entrust to a child? From the outside it is only a small flat rectangle, nothing much to look at. But when it is opened, Kay sees inside ". . . what he took to be a book, the leaves of which were all chased and worked with multitudinous figures, and the effect it gave him was that of staring into a wood."[33] The box that reveals one wonderful and sometimes also frightening scene after another, and gives one the power to travel in time and space, is in fact a book—or rather, all books. And the person who owns it has the power to bring the world to life through imagination; that is, he or she is a writer, or a child.

Masefield's literary sympathies were wide: he loved most of English poetry from its beginnings through the end of the nineteenth century, and he admired both Yeats and Frost. But he did not care for T. S. Eliot, and disliked most contemporary American poetry. Is it too far-fetched to point out that in *The Box of Delights, or When the Wolves Were Running*, the great danger is that the box may fall into the hands of a mercenary, wolfish American wizard?

In the book, at least, the danger is averted. Cole Hawlings gets his Box of Delights back at the end of the story with the help of Kay Harker, who is both Masefield's childhood self in the 1880s, portrayed in *The Midnight Folk*, and the child who survives within him in 1935. Magically or not, Masefield kept or regained his power to travel imaginatively in time and space, as a child does. He went on in the next few years to publish some of his most successful historical novels, including *Dead Ned* and *Live and Kicking Ned*, which many critics consider his best. Unfortunately, though, he never again wrote juvenile fiction. But he left to us, our children, and many children not yet born, four original and remarkable tales.

MOOMINTROLL AND HIS FRIENDS

To many Americans, Finland seems a strange and remote country. When they think of it, they imagine a largely empty landscape: snow-covered forests, gray rocky shores, icy lakes, and freezing rivers pass before their inner eyes to the accompaniment of the melancholy tone poems of Sibelius. Some, though, have another, more friendly and intimate vision of Finland. Because they know the stories of Tove Jansson, they imagine the country as bright with birds and flowers, and inhabited by fantastic and delightful creatures: the Moomintroll family and their sometimes charming, sometimes eccentric and difficult neighbors, so different from us in appearance yet so much like people we already know.

Today, Moomintroll is famous almost all over the world; his adventures have been translated into thirty-three languages. In Finland there is now a Moomin World theme park, and in England he has been the hero of a comic strip and a television series. But in America, for a long time, he was unknown. Now, however, his adventures are available here.

Tove Jansson, the creator of Moomintroll, who died in July 2001, was probably the best-known writer in Finland—not only for her children's books, but for her stories and novels for adults, one of which, *Sun City*, is set in an upmarket retirement home in Florida. She was also a successful artist who illustrated her own work with deceptively simple line drawings. Because of this we know exactly how her characters looked to their creator, something that is rare in stories for children past kindergarten age.

Jansson was born in 1914 of Swedish-speaking parents who had settled in Helsinki. Both were artists; her father, Viktor, was a well-known sculptor. Her mother, Signe, was a gifted illustrator who also designed two hundred Finnish stamps, and a famous storyteller. Tove Jansson inherited their talents. At fifteen she entered art school; later she studied in Germany, Italy, France, and London. Her first, brief Moomintroll story appeared in 1945. It was followed the next year by *Comet in Moominland*, the first of nine full-length Moomin books. Jansson, who never married, spent part of each year in Helsinki and the rest on a remote and beautiful island in the Gulf of Finland, where her family had gone in the summers since she was a small child. The island appears both in her adult stories and in *Moominpappa at Sea* (1954).

The author of the only book about Tove Jansson in English has compared the world of Moomintroll to that of A. A. Milne's *Winnie-the-Pooh*.[1] There is something to be said for this connection, though Jansson, by her own account, did not read the Pooh books until long after she had created Moomintroll. Perhaps the resemblances between the two series are the result of what a folklorist would call polygenesis: similar human situations tend to produce similar stories.

Tove Jansson's characters, like Milne's, are highly individual creatures, part human and part animal and part pure invention, living in a remote and peaceful rural world. Jansson's simple language, comic gift, and down-to-earth relation of odd events all recall Milne; and so does her love of the countryside and the high value she places on affection and good manners. Like Milne, she is a humanist; and also like him, though she writes for children, she deals with universal issues.

Some of Jansson's characters also recall Milne's. Her hero, Moomintroll, shares with Pooh his good nature, love of adventure, and innocent trustfulness. Though on first glance Moomintroll suggests a toy hippopotamus, his plump, pear-shaped body, short legs and arms, stand-up ears, and quizzical expression also make him look rather like E. H. Shepard's drawings of Pooh. Perhaps, though, it is not so much that they resemble each other as that both of them look like small children.

In Tove Jansson's earliest books Moomin, like Pooh, has a small and timid companion. Moomin's friend is called Sniff, and somewhat resembles a kangaroo. Sniff, however, is a less attractive character than Piglet. He is self-centered and dazzled by wealth, and in later books he becomes less prominent and finally disappears.

Misabel, who appears in *Moominsummer Madness* (1954), initially seems like a female version of Eeyore. ("Everything's gone wrong for me, simply everything," she declares on her first appearance.)[2] But whereas Eeyore remains perpetually gloomy, Misabel's self-dramatization of her own unhappiness is eventually transformed into theatrical talent, and she becomes the leading lady of a floating theater. In Tova Jansson's books, unlike Milne's, it is possible for characters to change.

There are also important differences between Moomintroll's world and that of Pooh. The setting of Milne's books is limited: a few acres of Sussex downs and woods. The Moonintroll landscape, on the other hand, stretches from the Lonely Mountains in the north and east to the villages south of Moomin Valley and the remote islands of the western sea. The world of Moomintroll is also less sheltered than that of Pooh. It contains parks and or-

phanages and prisons and astronomical observatories, light-
houses and telephones and fishing boats. It is much subject to
natural disasters: not only floods and high winds (which also occur in Milne), but violent snowstorms, deadly cold, earthquakes,
the eruption of a volcano, and a near-collision with a comet.
The difference between the climates of southern England and
Finland is also reflected in the books. Tove Jansson's characters
spend a lot of time simply trying to keep warm and dry.

Another and perhaps central difference between Milne's
world and Jansson's is that the Pooh stories depict an ideal society of friends, while the Moomintroll tales portray an ideal family. And whereas Milne's world is ruled by a male, Christopher
Robin, Moomin Valley clearly centers around Moominmamma.

Milne's model for the world of Pooh, apparently, was the
boys' school run by his father. All his characters are male, with
the exception of the fussily maternal Kanga, who can be seen as
the school nurse or matron. Jansson's stories, on the other hand,
contain many strongly individualized female characters. It must
be admitted, however, that this is true mainly of her later books.
In the first two tales of the series, the only female besides Moominmamma is the timid and featherbrained Snork Maiden. Though
she is fond of Moomintroll (whom she almost exactly resembles
except for her bangs), the Snork Maiden is mainly interested in
her own appearance and in clothes and jewelry.

In the later Moominland books, however, there are several
independent, brave, and attractive female characters, including
Mymble, Little My, and Too-Ticky. Instead of displaying the
stereotyped vanity and flightiness of the Snork Maiden, they are
more rational and detached than the male characters. Little My,
especially, is almost frighteningly cool. In appearance she resembles a plump little girl with a blond topknot, and though brave,
resourceful, intelligent, and psychologically perceptive, she is not
especially affectionate and seems to have no need for other

people. She also has no illusions about herself. In *Moominland Midwinter* (1957), when a little squirrel freezes to death, Moomintroll remarks that Little My doesn't feel sorry. "No," she agrees. "I can't. I'm always either glad or angry."[3]

Too-Ticky, another semihuman character, though as independent and practical as Little My, is more complex. Jansson has said that Too-Ticky was based on a close friend, the artist Tuulikki Pietila, whom she met in 1950 when she was feeling overworked and depressed. It was Tuulikki Pietila, she says, who taught her to have a more relaxed attitude toward life and to take things as they came. This is what Too-Ticky teaches Moomintroll in *Moominland Midwinter*, when he leaves the cozy house in which his family is hibernating and ventures out into the Finnish winter for the first time in his life. With Too-Ticky's encouragement he gradually begins to enjoy himself: he learns to ski and sees the Northern Lights.

When the first book in the series, *Comet in Moominland* (1946), appeared, Finland was just emerging from the dark years of World War II, during which the country was invaded by Russia and occupied by Germany. It is perhaps no surprise that the book tells of a difficult and dangerous time. In the course of the story, Moomintroll and his friends discover that a huge comet is approaching the earth. Gradually the rivers and oceans dry up; the world becomes hotter and hotter and darker and darker; there are tornadoes and plagues of grasshoppers. What keeps the story from being frightening or depressing is Moomintroll's optimism and love of adventure, and his confidence that whatever happens, Moominmamma will be equal to it.

In this book, as in those that follow, Moominmamma is the stable center of the story. She is the perfect mother: always kind, understanding, giving, and forgiving, an unending source of warmth and love and food. It is she who solves problems, gives advice, comforts the distressed, and generally holds the family together. Moominmamma believes that "all nice things are good for you,"[4] and wherever she is, even on a desert island or in the midst of a disaster, there is lots to eat and drink: raspberry juice, pancakes with homemade jam, birthday cake, blueberry pie, coffee, and sandwiches. Tove Jansson has said that Moominmamma is based upon her mother, Signe, whose stories were the beginning of the Moomintroll tales.

Moominmamma cares not only for her family but for any stray creature that wanders onto the scene. In *Tales from Moominvalley* (1995) she takes in a little girl so badly abused that she has become invisible. Moominmamma, with the help of her grandmother's old book of Household Remedies, gradually cures her. In *Moominpappa at Sea* she also manages to overcome the hysteria and confusion of a former lighthouse keeper who has had what seems like a nervous breakdown, and is described as "not a human being at all . . . more like a plant or a shadow."[5]

Moominpappa, on the other hand, is a somewhat ambiguous figure. Though he is an excellent craftsman, he is somewhat dreamy and self-preoccupied. He has a continual need to feel important, to be recognized by the world, and to think of himself as in charge. This leads him first to write his memoirs—published as *The Exploits of Moominpappa* (1952)—and later to insist that the whole family leave Moominvalley and go to live on a small island far out in the ocean.

The story of this move is recounted in one of Tove Jansson's best and most perceptive books, *Moominpappa at Sea*. (The original Swedish title does not have the double connotation of the English one, but it is certainly apt.) The story begins one afternoon, when

Moominpappa was walking about in his garden feeling at a loss. He had no idea what to do with himself, because it

seemed everything there was to be done had already been
done or was being done by somebody else.[6]

He does not enjoy or even practice his hobbies any longer. As
Tove Jansson puts it,

> Moominpappa . . . had got his fishing-rod on his birthday a
> couple of years before and it was a very fine one. But some-
> times it stood in its corner in a slightly unpleasant way, as
> though reminding him that it was for catching fish.[7]

Moominpappa, like many suburban fathers with a rather meaningless job, or none at all, is bored and depressed. He consoles
himself by going into the garden and looking at his family reflected in a crystal ball, which

> made them all seem incredibly small, . . . and all their move-
> ments seem forlorn and aimless.
>   Moominpappa liked this. It was his evening game. It made
> him feel that they all needed protection, that they were at the
> bottom of a deep sea that only he knew about.[8]

When he declares that they are all going to move to the island, Moominmamma accepts it philosophically. "Now the
proper thing to do was that they should begin an entirely new
life, and that Moominmamma should provide everything they
needed, look after them and protect them," she thinks.[9] In fact,
once the family reaches the island and moves into a deserted
lighthouse, it is Moominmamma who looks after everyone and
solves the problems that arise, though Moominpappa does finally catch some—indeed, far too many—fish.
   Living on the island is difficult, especially as the weather turns
colder. Moominpappa becomes bewildered and confused, even
mildly paranoid. Moominmamma does her best, but sometimes
she has to retreat into the garden she has painted on the walls

of the lighthouse. The book ends happily, but it is reassuring to learn that eventually the family will return to Moominvalley.

One of Tova Jansson's most remarkable creations is her gallery of strange and eccentric characters, many of whom, in spite of their odd appearance, are familiar human types. The strangest species in Moominland are the Hattifatteners—mobs of pale, anonymous beings who resemble stalks of white asparagus with rudimentary arms and hands. They cannot hear or speak to Moomintroll and his friends, and are "interested only in traveling onwards, as far as possible."[10] The Hattifatteners irresistibly suggest mobs of packaged foreign tourists, and it is not surprising that at one of the times when Moominpappa is feeling especially restless and dissatisfied at home, he goes on a voyage with them. During a thunderstorm they suddenly come to life and start swaying back and forth, and Moominpappa becomes disillusioned. "They were heavily charged but hopelessly locked up," he thinks. "They didn't feel, they didn't think, they could only seek."[11]

The Hemulen, on the other hand, represent established authority, organization, the adult world. They look like larger, more rectangular Moomins in human dress (though all Hemulen, both male and female, wear skirts). They are officials, policemen, park-keepers, and managers of orphanages. Some are oppressive and hateful, others merely pathetic. The Hemulen in *Moominvalley in November*, for example,

> spent the whole day arranging, organizing and directing things from morning till night! All around him there were people living slipshod and aimless lives, wherever he looked there was something to be put right, and he worked his fingers to the bone trying to get them to see how they ought to live.[12]

Nevertheless he is chronically tired and bored, and feels "that days passed without anything of importance happening."[13] Other

Hemulen do not try to organize anyone, but are obsessed with collecting butterflies or stamps, and none of them are any help about the house or in times of trouble.

Fillyjonks also seem to represent adult authority, but of a less oppressive kind. Most of them are female, just as most Hemulen are male. Fillyjonks, who slightly resemble grey-hounds, tend to be silly and fussy, to fear dirt and insects. They are house-proud, attached to their possessions and constantly cleaning. They rigidly observe the rules of polite behavior, and often invite relatives and neighbors they really dislike to meals. But sometimes, at these depressing social events, the mask slips:

"We are so small and insignificant," [one Fillyjonk suddenly whispers to a guest] "and so are our teacakes and carpets and all those things, you know, and still they're so important, but always they're threatened by mercilessness. . . .

"Tornadoes, whirlwinds, sand-storms. . . . Flood waves that carry houses away. . . . But most of all I'm talking about myself and my fears, even if I know that's not done. I know every-thing will turn out badly. I think about that all the time."[14]

There are also many characters in Moominland who do not represent a species. There is, for instance, the Muskrat, who an-nounces that he is a philosopher (an illustration shows that he has recently been reading or pretending to read Spengler). The Muskrat spends most of his time in a hammock, waiting for other people (usually Moominmamma) to bring him lunch. "It's all a matter of thinking," he says. "I sit and think about how un-necessary everything is."[15] When the Muskrat absentmindedly sits on Moomintroll's birthday cake, he is unaware of it. "I don't bother myself over things like cakes," he says. "I don't see them, taste them, or feel them in any way, ever."[16] The accompanying illustration, however, shows the Muskrat consuming a large piece of squashed cake.

One of the most remarkable things about Tove Jansson is her sympathy for her most unlikable characters. In *Moomin-valley in November* (1971), the last and most complex of the series, a Hemulen and a Fillyjonk move into the Moomin family's deserted house while they are away on the island. The Hemulen tries to play the part of Moominpappa, with limited success, especially when he insists on teaching everyone to ski. The Fillyjonk, who doesn't really like children, attempts to replace Moominmamma. Though Jansson makes fun of the Hemulen and the Fillyjonk, she also pities them and even seems to respect their clumsy efforts. By the end of the series, Jansson has gotten to the point where she can sympathize even with her most difficult and frightening creation. This is the Groke, a strange, large, dark, longhaired, mound-shaped creature with huge staring eyes that seems to represent depression and despair. The Groke is a kind of walking manifestation of Scandinavian gloom: everything the Groke touches dies, and the ground freezes wherever she sits. If she stays in one place for an hour, the earth becomes permanently barren. "You felt that she was terribly evil and would wait for ever," Jansson says in one of the earlier books.[17]

But even the normally self-centered Sniff can sympathize with the Groke. "Think how lonely the Groke is because nobody likes her, and she hates everybody," he says.[18] At first the best anyone can do is get rid of her temporarily. But finally, in *Moominpappa at Sea*, it is Moomintroll himself who tames the Groke. He comes with a lantern every night to the beach where she sits freezing the sand and making "a thin sound, something like humming and whistling together. . . . after a while Moomintroll felt that it was inside his head, behind his eyes."[19] One night he sees the Groke dance, swaying "slowly and heavily from side to side, waving her skirts up and down until they looked like dry, wrinkled bat's wings."[20] When she leaves after-

ward, the sand where she has sat is no longer frozen. Perhaps
Tove Jansson is saying that we must become familiar with our
darkest moods, and even encourage them to express themselves.

A final and very interesting Moominland character is Snufkin,
one of the most human-looking figures in the books. He is a
solitary fellow with an old green hat and a mouth organ who
seems to represent the artist—perhaps Tove Jansson herself.
Snufkin is Moomintroll's best friend, but he is not always around.
He goes south in the winter, and sometimes he prefers to be
alone and think of tunes.

On his first appearance, in *Comet in Moominland*, Snufkin is
an anonymous wanderer; but later he (like Tove Jansson) has
become locally famous. In one story, "The Spring Tune," his cre-
ative efforts are disrupted by the arrival of a fan, a small, fuzzy,
wide-eyed creature called, perhaps not accidentally, "the creep."
"Just think of it," the creep says. "I'll be the creep who has sat
by Snufkin's camp-fire. I'll never forget that."[21]

When Snufkin, becoming impatient with the adulation, remarks, "You can't ever be really free if you admire somebody
too much," the creep does not hear him.

"I know you know everything," the little creep prattled on,
edging closer still. "I know you've seen everything. You're
right in everything you say, and I'll always try to become as
free as you are."[22]

In the last story of the series, Snufkin, who has been search-
ing for a new tune, is lying in his tent trying to fall asleep. But he
cannot stop thinking about the other characters in the story.

Whatever he did, there they were in his tent, all the time, the
Heumlen's immobile eyes, and Fillyjonk lying weeping on
her bed, and Toft who just kept quiet and stared at the

ground, and old Grandpa Grumble all confused . . . they were everywhere, right inside his head.[23]

Some authors cannot forget their characters even after the book is finished. Perhaps this is how Tove Jansson came to feel in the years when she tried to turn to adult fiction, but found herself instead writing a final, brilliant Moominland tale.

DR. SEUSS COMES BACK

ᴍᴏʀᴇ than ten years after his death, Theodor Seuss Geisel, known to millions as Dr. Seuss, remains the most popular juvenile author in America. Almost everyone now under fifty was brought up on his books and cartoons, and even those who didn't hear the stories read aloud probably saw them on TV or video, or met his fantastic characters at school. One of Seuss's greatest gifts to children was the series of first-grade readers he wrote for Random House to replace the conventional "Dick and Jane" stories with their white middle-class suburban families, and dull suburban happenings. In *The Cat in the Hat* (1957) and *Green Eggs and Ham* (1960) Seuss managed to create wonderful, innovative, crazily comic tales with a minimum vocabulary. (*The Cat in the Hat* uses only 220 words.) These books, and their sequels, made learning fun for kids from every kind of background, and revolutionized the teaching of reading. Their inventive energy and their freedom from class and race norms made Dick and Jane look dull, prissy, limited, and totally outdated.

What made it all even more wonderful was that Dr. Seuss's

life was a classic American success story. As a child in Spring-field, Massachusetts, he had the kind of luck most kids only dream of: his father was in charge of the local zoo. Theodor could visit it whenever he liked, and go everywhere behind the scenes. When he grew up he became a kind of zookeeper him-self: the inventor and ringmaster of an ever-expanding mena-gerie of fantastic comic creatures: Sneeches and Lunks and Yooks and Zooks, the Lorax, and *The Grinch Who Stole Christmas*. One of his early books was even called *If I Ran the Zoo* (1950).

Seuss began as a cartoonist and advertising artist; his "Quick, Henry, the Flit!" drawings showing a citizen attacked by giant in-sects, half-comic and half-threatening, were strikingly original and widely reproduced. In 1941–42 he also drew more than four hundred political cartoons for the short-lived New York liberal newspaper *PM,* full of the strange birds and beasts for which he would later be famous. But Seuss's first children's book, the bril-liant *And to Think That I Saw It on Mulberry Street* (1937), was re-jected by at least twenty-seven publishers; editors complained that it contained "no moral or message" and would not help in "transforming children into good citizens."[1] The book was finally taken on by an old college friend, Marshall McClintock, who had just become the juvenile editor of Vanguard Press.[2]

Though publishers may be slow, readers—especially chil-dren—are usually quick to recognize genius. *Mulberry Street* was a hit, and so were all its successors. Though Seuss died in 1991, most of his books are still in print, and they have been translated into dozens of languages.

Why didn't editors see at once what a winner Seuss would be? Partly because of his artistic style, which was unabashedly cartoonlike and exaggerated in an era when children's book il-lustration was supposed to be pretty and realistic. Perhaps even more because of the content of his stories, especially their en-couragement of wild invention and, even worse, the suggestion that it might be politic to conceal one's fantasy life from parents.

Children in the 1930s and 1940s were supposed to be learning about the real world, not wasting their time on fantasies and daydreams, and they were encouraged to tell their parents everything.

Marco, the hero of *And to Think That I Saw It on Mulberry Street,* is warned by his father at the start of the book to "stop telling such outlandish tales" about what he sees on the way home from school. Yet the very next day Marco's imagination turns a horse and wagon, by gradual stages, into a full-blown parade with elephants, giraffes, a brass band, and a plane showering colored confetti—all portrayed by Seuss with immense verve and enthusiasm. Marco arrives home in a state of euphoria:

> I swung 'round the corner
> And dashed through the gate,
> I ran up the steps
> And I felt simply GREAT!
> FOR I HAD A STORY THAT NO ONE COULD BEAT!
> And to think that I saw it on Mulberry Street!

Then he is quizzed by his father about what he has seen. His reply is evasive:

> "Nothing," I said, growing red as a beet,
> "But a plain horse and wagon on Mulberry Street."

The message that it is sometimes, perhaps always, best to conceal one's inner imaginative life from adults reappears in *The Cat in the Hat* (1957). Here "Sally and I," two children alone and bored on a rainy day, are visited by the eponymous Cat. He proceeds to totally wreck their house, causing first excitement and then panic. (What will their mother say when she gets home?) Finally he puts everything back in place. The kids—and not only those in the story, but those who read it—have vicariously

given full scope to their destructive impulses without guilt or
consequences. When their mother returns and asks what
they've been doing, there is a strong suggestion that they might
not level with her:

> Should we tell her about it?
> Now, what SHOULD we do? Well . . .
> What would YOU do
> If your mother asked YOU?

In both these tales the children whose imagination trans-
forms the world are abashed or secretive when confronted with
possible adult disapproval. More often, however, Seuss lets fancy
run free without equivocation or apology. A whole series of
books from *McElligot's Pool* (1947) through *On Beyond Zebra!*
(1955) and *If I Ran the Circus* (1956) celebrates the wildest flights
of fancy. They usually begin in familiar surroundings, then move
into an invented world where the scenery recalls the exotic landscapes of Krazy Kat comics. There, just as Seuss's Elephant-Bird,
Tufted Gustard, and Spotted Atrocious defy natural history, so
his buildings and roads and mountains defy gravity. As the critic
Philip Nel has pointed out, one effect of this kind of semisurreal
nonsense is to suggest to children that the limited physical and
linguistic world constructed by adults is not the only possible
one.[3] Seuss, as is well known, often thought of himself as a child,
and once remarked, "I've always had a mistrust of adults."[4]

Though these stories are full of euphoric vitality, there is occasionally something unsatisfying about them. Seuss's verbal inventions can become as shaky and overblown as the structures
in his drawings. At the end of many of his books the elaborate
language often does collapse. There is an abrupt return to simple diction, and a simple, realistic final illustration implicitly declares that Seuss's protagonist was only fantasizing.

Innovative as he was, Seuss can also be seen as squarely in

the tradition of American popular humor. His strenuous and constant energy, his delight in invention and nonsense recall the boasts and exaggerations of the nineteenth-century tall tale, with its reports of strange animals like the Snipe and the Side-Winder. Seuss brought this manner and these materials up to date for a generation raised on film and TV cartoons. And, though most of the time he addresses himself almost exclusively to children, he includes occasional jokes for adults. In *If I Ran the Zoo* (1950), for instance, the hero plans to bring a Seersucker back alive; he will also "go down to the Wilds of Nantucket/And capture a family of Lunks in a bucket." According to the illustrations, the Seersucker is a foolish, shaggy, flower-eating animal with what looks like a red bow tie, while Lunks are pale, big-eyed creatures with blond topknots, captured with the help of beach buggies.

Parents as well as children seem to be addressed in *One Fish Two Fish Red Fish Blue Fish* (1960) in which two kids find a very large uncomfortable-looking tusked sea monster. They exult:

> Look what we found
> in the park
> in the dark.
> We will take him home.
> We will call him Clark.
> He will live at our house.
> He will grow and grow.
> Will our mother like this?
> We don't know.

Seuss is not only in favor of the free-ranging imagination; in many of his books there is a strong liberal, even antiestablishment moral. Some critics have even seen *The Cat in the Hat Comes Back* (1958) as a satire of Cold War paranoia, in which the Cat, with the help of an A–Z series of smaller cats, spreads bright-pink paint all over the house in a mockery of the current fear of Communist takeover. The narrator and his sister, Sally, become more and more anxious about this, but finally when Little Cat Z raises his hat, releasing something called Voom (perhaps a benign version of the atomic bomb), the pinko/red menace is magically removed.[5]

In other books by Seuss, as in the classic folktale, pride and prejudice are ridiculed, and autocratic rule is overturned. In *Yertle the Turtle* (1958) Mack, who is bottom turtle on the live totem pole that elevates King Yertle, objects to the system:

> I know, up on top you are seeing great sights,
> But down at the bottom, we, too, should have rights. . . .
> Besides, we need food. We are starving!

So he burps and upsets the whole stack, turning Yertle into King of the Mud. In *Bartholomew and the Oobleck* (1949) another overreaching ruler, dissatisfied with the monotony of the weather, commands his magicians to cause something more interesting than rain or snow to fall from the sky. He gets a sticky, smelly substance that, though it appears as green, is clearly excrement ("You're sitting in oobleck up to your chin.") It does not disappear until the king admits that the whole thing was his own fault.

In *Horton Hatches the Egg* (1940) and *Horton Hears a Who* (1954) a charitable and self-sacrificing elephant protects the rights of the unborn and of small nations and obscure individuals in spite of the ridicule and scorn of his friends, because "A person's a person, no matter how small." There are limits to charity in Seuss, however. *Thidwick the Big-Hearted Moose* (1948) allows his horns to become the refuge of an overwhelming number of visiting animals and bugs, repeating wearily, "A host, above all, must be nice to his guests." Luckily, just when he reaches the limits of his endurance and is being pursued by hunters, his antlers fall off and he escapes. His guests end up stuffed and mounted on the wall of the Harvard Club, "as they should be." It is perhaps stretching a point to suggest that the book conveys an anti-immigration message, but perhaps not.

For years Seuss's tales were hailed by experts as a wonderful way to teach children not only reading but moral values as well. Meanwhile, however, a couple of them ran into opposition. In 1989 logging companies in Northern California went after *The Lorax* (1971). In this story a greedy Once-ler and his relatives move into an area of natural beauty and proceed to chop down all the colorful Truffula Trees in order to manufacture Thneeds, which resemble unattractive hairy pink underwear. Soon the sky is choked with smog and the water with something called Gluppity-Glup. Though Seuss said the book was about conservation in general, the loggers saw it as blatant propaganda and agitated to have it banned from the local school's required reading list. "Our kids are being brainwashed. We've got to stop this crap right now!" shouted their ad in the local paper, taking much the same belligerent antienvironmental tone as the Once-ler himself does when criticized:

> I yelled at the Lorax, "Now Listen here, Dad!
> All you do is yap-yap and say 'Bad! Bad! Bad! Bad!'
> Well, I have my rights, sir, and I'm telling *you*
> I intend to go on doing just what I do!
> And for your information, you Lorax, I'm figgering
>   on biggering
>   and BIGGERING
>   and BIGGERING
>   and BIGGERING,
> turning MORE Truffula Trees into Thneeds
> which everyone, EVERYONE, EVERYONE needs!"

The Butter Battle Book (1984), a fable about the arms race, also provoked unfavorable comment. Like Swift's tale of the Big- and Little-Endians who went to war over how to open an egg, it begins with a meaningless difference in domestic habits. Two groups of awkward-looking flightless birds, the Yooks and the Zooks, live side by side. The Yooks eat their bread butter-side up, the Zooks prefer it butter-side down. They become more and more suspicious of each other, and finally a member of the Zook Border Patrol with the rather Slavic-sounding name of VanItch´ fires his slingshot. Escalation begins: more and more complicated weapons are developed by the Boys in the Back Room ("TOPEST, SECRETEST, BRAIN NEST!" says the sign on their door), until both sides possess the means of total destruction. Unlike most of Seuss's books, this one doesn't end reassuringly, but with the child narrator asking anxiously: "Who's going to drop it? / Will *you* . . . ? Or will *he* . . . ?" *The New York Times Book Review* considered the story "too close to contemporary international reality for comfort," while *The New Republic*, somewhat missing the point, complained that the issues between our real-life Zooks and Yooks were more important than methods of buttering bread.

Other, perhaps more relevant criticisms might be made today of Seuss's work. For one thing, there is the almost total lack of female protagonists; indeed, many of his stories have no female characters at all. *You're Only Old Once!* (1986), a cheerfully rueful tale about the medical woes of a senior citizen, which was on *The New York Times* best-seller list for months, is no exception. It contains one female receptionist (only her arm is visible) and one female nurse, plus a male patient, a male orderly, twenty-one male doctors and technicians, and one male fish.

The typical Seuss hero is a small boy or a male animal; when little girls appear, they play silent secondary roles. The most memorable female in his entire oeuvre is the despicable Mayzie, the lazy bird who callously traps Horton into sitting on her egg so that she can fly off to Palm Beach. Another unattractive bird, Gertrude McFuzz in *Yertle the Turtle and Other Stories* (1958), is vain, envious, greedy, stupid, and fashion-mad. She gorges on magic berries to increase the size of her tail, and ends up unable to walk.

Seuss's little girls, unlike his boys, are not encouraged to expand their imaginations very far. In "The Gunk That Got Thunk," one of the tales in *I Can Lick 30 Tigers Today!* (1969), this is made clear. The narrator relates how his little sister customarily used her "Thinker-Upper" to "think up friendly little things / With smiles and fuzzy fur." One day, however, she got bored: she speeded up the process and created a giant Gunk:

> He was greenish.
> Not too cleanish.
> And he sort of had bad breath.

She tries to unthink him, but fails; meanwhile the Gunk gets on the phone and runs up a three-hundred-dollar long-distance bill describing recipes. Finally he is unthunk with the help of the narrator, who then gives his sister

> Quite a talking-to
> About her Thinker-Upper.
>
> NOW . . .
> She only
> Thinks up fuzzy things
> In the evening after supper.

The suggestion is that females must not be ambitious even in imagination. They have weak minds; their alter egos are greedy and extravagant and spend too much time on the phone.

The only book by Seuss with a female protagonist, *Daisy-Head Mayzie,* was based on a never-produced film-animation script found among his papers after his death. It was published in 1995 with uneven Seuss-type verses and Seuss-type illustrations, some apparently by an anonymous collaborator. Many of the drawings seem to be copies of illustrations from other Seuss books. (The Cat in the Hat, who is not mentioned in the story, appears on several pages.) Plump, blond, pink-frocked Mayzie is an essentially passive and frightened character, more victim than heroine—a sort of juvenile Marilyn Monroe.

After a flower sprouts on the top of her head, Mayzie loses her anonymity. Her doctor wants to make her the subject of a research grant; the mayor mentions her in speeches; eventually she becomes a dazed celebrity, used by her agent and by cynical politicians. She is famous not for what she can do or create, like the hero of *If I Ran the Zoo,* but for the way she looks.[6]

Mayzie goes on TV and inspires commercial spin-offs:

> Daisy-Head burgers,
> And Daisy-Head drinks,
> Daisy-Head stockings,
> And Daisy-Head sinks.

But Mayzie is not happy with her money and fame; instead, like some real-life celebrities, she becomes obsessed with the idea that nobody loves her. To find out for sure she begins picking the petals off her daisy, and they come up with a positive answer. Mayzie returns, daisy-less and happy, to her family and friends and school. Now and then, though "practically never," the flower briefly—and apparently harmlessly—reappears.

Seuss's most popular recent book, *Oh, the Places You'll Go!* (1990), which by July 2001 had been on *The New York Times* best-seller list for 207 weeks, also has a male hero. But in other ways the story was a departure for him. "The theme is limitless horizons and hope," Seuss, then eighty-six years old, told an interviewer; and the blurb describes the book as a "joyous ode to personal fulfillment." But what it really reads like is the yuppie dream—or nightmare—of the 1990s in cartoon form.

At the beginning of the story the standard Seuss boy hero appears in what looks like the cartoon version of a large, clean, modern city (featureless yellow buildings, wide streets, tidy plots of grass). But under this city, as any urbanite might expect, are unpleasant, dangerous things—in this case, long-necked green monsters who put their heads out of manholes. Seeing them, Seuss's hero, "too smart to go down any not-so-good street," heads "straight out of town."

At first everything goes well; he acquires an escort of four purple (Republican?) elephants and rises in the world, joining "the high fliers / who soar to high heights." The narrative is encouraging:

> You'll pass the whole gang and you'll soon take the lead.
> Wherever you fly, you'll be the best of the best.
> Wherever you go, you will top all the rest.

In the accompanying illustration Seuss's hero is carried by a pink and yellow balloon high over fields and mountains; his competitors, in less colorful balloons, lag behind at a lower altitude.

Then comes the first disaster: the balloon is snagged by a dead tree and deflated. The boy's "gang" doesn't stop for him—as presumably he wouldn't for them—and he finds himself first in a Lurch and then in a Slump, the latter portrayed as a dismal rocky seminighttime landscape with giant blue slugs draped about in a Dali-like manner. Doggedly, he goes on and comes to a city full of arches and domes that looks rather Near Eastern,

> . . . where the streets are not marked.
> Some windows are lighted. But mostly they're darked.

Turning aside (in the light of the current political situation, an excellent choice), he continues "down long wiggled roads" toward what Seuss calls The Waiting Place. Here the sky is inky black, and many discouraged-looking people and creatures are standing around:

> . . . waiting, perhaps, for their Uncle Jake
> or a pot to boil, or a Better Break.

For the energetic, ever-striving young American, this is a fate worse than death, and it is vigorously rejected:

> NO!
> That's not for you!
>
> Somehow you'll escape all that waiting and staying.
> You'll find the bright places where Boom Bands
>   are playing.

Seuss's hero is next seen riding on another purple elephant in a procession of elephants, on his way to further solitary triumphs.

> Oh, the places you'll go. There is fun to be done!
> There are points to be scored. There are games
>   to be won. . . .
> *Fame!* You'll be famous as famous can be,
> With the whole wide world watching you win on TV.

In the accompanying picture some kind of fantasy football or lacrosse is being played—our hero kicking off from the back of his elephant, the other contestants on foot. But almost immediately this success is undercut:

> Except when they don't.
> Because, sometimes, they won't.
>
> I'm afraid that *some* times
> you'll play lonely games too.
> Games you can't win
> 'cause you'll play against you.

Clearly, the most dangerous enemy of the celebrity is his own doubt and self-dislike. The illustration shows a totally insecure-looking fantasy version of a Hollywood hillside mansion, where the hero is shooting baskets alone. Seuss assumes, no doubt quite properly, that in any career devoted to success, competition, and fame, "Alone will be something / you'll be quite a lot," and that often "you won't want to go on."

But his hero, of course, does go on, meeting a number of comical and/or frightening monsters. Seuss predicts

> You'll get mixed up
> With many strange birds as you go.

The strange birds, who all look alike, are shown against another totally black background, some marching upward to the right with smiles, others plodding downward to the left with depressed expressions. The message here seems to be that it is a mistake to commit oneself to any organization; instead one must

> Step with care and great tact
> and remember that Life's
> a Great Balancing Act.

This is followed by the happy climax, in which Seuss's hero is even more triumphant than before:

> And will you succeed?
> Yes! You will, indeed!
> (98 and 3/4 percent guaranteed.)
>
> KID, YOU'LL MOVE MOUNTAINS!

This promise is depicted literally in the illustration: if we choose to take it that way, we might assume that Seuss's kid has become a property developer, like so many California celebrities.

In one or two of Seuss's earlier books, similar dreams of money and fame occur. Gerald McGrew, for instance, imagines that

The whole world will say, Young McGrew's made his mark.
He's built a zoo better than Noah's whole Ark! . . .

"Wow!" They'll all cheer,
"What this zoo must be worth!"

This was written in 1950, when Seuss's own imaginary zoo had just begun to make his fortune. Later on, life wholly imitated art: his wild inventions, like those of his boy heroes—and, of course, in the end they are the same thing—made him fantastically rich and famous. It is difficult to estimate what Seuss's own zoo must be worth now; according to his publishers in 1990, more than two hundred million copies of his books had been sold world-wide, and many of them have been animated for television or adapted for the stage.

Gerald McGrew and Seuss's other early heroes were content simply to fantasize success. *Oh, the Places You'll Go!* has a different moral. Now happiness no longer lies in exercising one's imagination, achieving independence from tyrants, or helping weaker creatures as Horton does. It is equated with wealth, fame, and getting ahead of others. Moreover, anything less than absolute success is seen as failure—a well-known American delusion, and a very destructive one. There are also no personal relationships here except that of competition. Unlike most of Seuss's earlier protagonists, the hero has no friends and no family.

Who is buying this book, and why? Apparently it is a very popular college-graduation gift, and also often given to people who are changing jobs or careers. It is a pep talk, and meets the same need that is satisfied by those stiffly smiling financial experts who declare on television that any glitch in America's prosperity is a Gunk that will soon be unthunk, to be followed—On Beyond Zebra!—by even greater success.

HAROUN AND THE SEA OF STORIES

Behind many of the greatest and most joyful children's fantasies move the shadows of real and often unhappy events in their authors' lives. Many of Beatrix Potter's animals escape from claustrophobic domestic environments like that of her own respectably repressive Victorian parents. J. M. Barrie's Peter Pan, like Barrie himself, never attains maturity, and must borrow or steal other people's children for his playmates. And E. B. White, who as both a child and an adult was described as resembling a mouse, made the hero of *Stuart Little* a mouse born into a human family.

Salman Rushdie's remarkable new children's book belongs in this company. The only difference is that the experiences that lie behind *Haroun and the Sea of Stories* are nearly as fantastic as anything in the tale. Before the fact, who could have believed that a world-famous spiritual leader, the Ayatollah Khoumeni, would publicly exhort his millions of followers to murder a novelist in another country, and promise them eternal salvation should they succeed?

On the surface, *Haroun and the Sea of Stories* is a lively, wonderfully inventive comic tale with an updated Arabian Nights background and a happy ending. But it was begun at a time when Rushdie was hiding under police protection and in near despair about his own writing. As he told James Fenton:

> To attempt a work of fiction after what had happened to me wasn't easy. There were many times in the months after this began that I said to myself that I no longer wished to be a writer. I felt that everything I had put into the act of being a writer had failed. . . . [If] the whole planet thinks of you as a complete bastard, you wonder what it's about, what it was for, and why do it.[1]

What made Rushdie start writing again was a promise he had made to his son, Zafar ("Triumph" in Arabic), that when he had finished *The Satanic Verses* he would write a book that children could read.

> . . . then all this happened, and I was unable to do anything for him . . . there was this nine-year-old boy suddenly deprived of his father, and I thought there's only one promise to him that I can keep . . . it was the thing that brought me back to writing.[2]

The book is dedicated with an acrostic poem to his son, and its young protagonist, Haroun, is clearly based on him.

Haroun and the Sea of Stories follows the classic folktale pattern in which a young hero travels to strange lands to lift a spell on his native country or cure a parent of a fatal ailment. In the course of the story he is often aided by supernatural companions and confronts and defeats a wicked magician.

The hero of Rushdie's tale is the son of the famous storyteller

Rashid (a near anagram of "Rushdie") Kalifa ("Caliph"), who is known to his neighbors as the "Ocean of Notions." Rashid is able, like Orpheus, to command the fascinated attention not only of men and women and children, but also of birds and beasts. But "luck has a way of running out without the slightest warning."[3] One day Rashid's wife leaves him for a thin, whiny neighbor who hates stories; Rashid loses his gift and can only croak, "Ark, ark, ark."[4]

This affliction of speech, central to the book, is paralled by the affliction of the country, which is called Alifbay ("alphabet" in Hindustani). Most of the names in the book derive from this language, and a convenient glossary is provided at the end. It is worth checking this out, for as Rashid tells his son, "All names mean something." At the start of the book Haroun and his father live in "a sad city, the saddest of cities, a city so ruinously sad that it had forgotten its name. It stood by a mournful sea full of glumfish."[5]

Though it is unfortunate to have a name with dark connotations, it is even worse to have no name at all. Here, sorrow causes one to forget one's name and lose the ability to speak; and no wonder, considering the recent life of its author. Under how many false and forgettable names, in how many sad cities, I wonder, has Rushdie had to conceal himself since the publication of his much-praised and much-condemned novel *The Satanic Verses?*

The villian responsible for Rashid's affliction is the sinister tyrant of the dark land of Chup ("Silence"), Khattam-Shud, whose name means "completely finished" or "over and done with." He is "the Arch-Enemy of all stories, even of Language itself."[6] In appearance, however, he is not fearsome: he is "a skinny, scrawny, measly, weaselly, sniveling clerical type."[7] Khattam-Shud's fanatical followers have sworn a vow of silence, and are working round the clock to poison the Sea of Stories. Their country is not only dark and soundless, but freezing cold: "a place of shadows, of books that wear padlocks and tongues torn out."[8]

"But why do you hate stories so much?" Haroun asks when he finally confronts the tyrant. "Stories are fun."

"The world, however, is not for Fun. . . . The world is for Controlling," replies Khattam-Shud, who though he will allow no one else to speak, talks continually in a "dull, inflexionless voice." "And inside every single story, inside every Stream in the Ocean, there lies a world, a story-world, that I cannot Rule at all."[9]

Though there is darkness and silence at the center of Chup, most of *Haroun and the Sea of Stories* is full of a comic energy and lively verbal invention that recall L. Frank Baum's Oz books. Rushdie himself has acknowledged his debt to Baum. In a pamphlet on *The Wizard of Oz* published by the British Film Institute, he writes:

> When I first saw *The Wizard of Oz* it made a writer of me. Many years later, I began to devise the yarn that eventually became Haroun and the Sea of Stories, and felt strongly that if I could strike the right note it should be possible to write the tale in such a way as to make it of interest to "children from seven to seventy."[10]

In the course of his travels Haroun acquires three fantastical companions who, like Dorothy's, represent the animal, vegetable, and mineral kingdoms: IFF the Water Genie, who is semihuman; Mali, a "Floating Gardener First Class," made of seaweed; and Mr. Butt, a bus driver who later turns into Butt the Hoopoe, a mechanical bird with telepathic abilities.[11] Haroun visits several odd, self-contained communities like those in the Oz books: in Moody Land, for example, the climate is affected by the mental and emotional state of the inhabitants rather than vice versa. The book also contains a brave and enterprising girl character who disguises herself as a boy in order to join the Library army. "You think it's *easy* for a girl to get a job like this?" she asks Haroun. "Don't you know girls have to *fool people* every *day* of their *lives* if they want to get *anywhere?*"[12] Female readers will regret that this young feminist plays such a small part in the story, and even more that she goes by the ugly name of Blabbermouth.

There are other echoes from earlier children's classics. Rushdie's puns and anagrams, and his exuberant wordplay, suggest both *Alice in Wonderland* and Norton Juster's *The Phantom Tollbooth*.[13] The army (or "Library") of the good land of Gup ("Gossip" or "Nonsense") is composed of Pages in thin uniforms covered with writing, who are organized into Chapters and Volumes; its general is called Kitab ("Book" in Hindustani). Their love of free speech gives them an advantage over the silent soldiers of Chup whose "habits of secrecy had made them suspicious and distrustful of one another."[14]

Though it was composed in English by an author living in Britain, *Haroun and the Sea of Stories* is also in several ways a modern classic of Indian literature. Many of the characters speak a language that, though odd to Western ears, is typical of the English spoken in India. Suchismita Sen, in a perceptive analysis of the book, remarks that some of the dialogue in Haroun "resembles the English used by Indian newspapers during the nineteenth century, the language that was commonly called Babu English." It is characterized by the use of formal or official speech in conversation, even in crisis situations. Thus when the bus driver Mr. Butt begins to go faster and faster, causing his passengers "to hoot and howl with excitement and fear,"[15] his response sounds partly like a provincial newspaper and partly like an official proclamation:

"See here this bend, what a tight one!" Mr. Butt sang out. "Here, two weeks ago, occurred a major disaster. Bus plunged into gully, all persons killed, sixty–seventy lives minimum. God! Too sad! If you desire I can stop for taking of photographs.

"Yes, stop, stop," the passengers begged (anything to make him slow down), but Mr. Butt went even faster instead. "Too late," he yodeled gaily. "Already it is far behind. Requests must be more promptly made if I am to comply."[16]

In spite of all the dangers they face, in the end, of course, Haroun and his magical companions defeat Khattam-Shud and restore the Sea of Stories to health. As a reward, Haroun is given a single wish; what he asks for is that his native city may cease to be sad and may remember its name, which turns out to be Kahani ("Story"). His mother returns, and his father, Rashid, is again able to tell his wonderful tales.

Though *Haroun and the Sea of Stories* is sure to be enjoyed by children, it also contains pleasures for adults who might be reading the book aloud or even (why not?) to themselves. The well-known complication of the Stith Thompson index to Indo-European folktales is gently mocked when Haroun drinks from the Ocean of Story and finds himself in the middle of a variant of a classic tale type:

What Haroun was experiencing, though he didn't know it, was Princess Rescue Story Number s/1011/ZHT/420/41®xi.[17]

There is also a Shadow Warrior who can only speak in gestures, but coughs, "Gogogol . . . Kafkafka."[18] The extremely foolish and incompetent prince and the ugly princess of Gup recall Thackeray's burlesque fairy tale, *The Rose and the Ring*; but they may also remind some readers of the problems of the British royal family. ("After all," says one of Haroun's companions, "it's not as if we really let our crowned heads do anything very important around here.")[19] Another nod to the adult reader appears in the remark of the Floating Gardener that one of the ill effects of the poisoning of the Sea of Stories is that

> Certain popular romances have become just long lists of shopping expeditions. Children's stories also. For instance, there is an outbreak of talking helicopter anecdotes.[20]

Rushdie also pays tribute to the stories and films he loved as a child. Many of his episodes and characters recall the Arabian Nights tales, and the Plentimaw Fish ("there really are Plentimaw Fish in the Sea") who talk in rhymed doggerel are named Goopy and Bagda, after the comic heroes of Satyajit Ray Ray's popular film for children, *Goopy Gyne and Bagha Byne* (1969).

If there is one encouraging conclusion to be drawn from the problems of Salman Rushdie, it is that literature has power—so much power that it is dreaded by dictators. A single storyteller like Rashid is more dangerous to a tyrant than an army. "What starts with *stories* ends with spying," says Khattam-Shud. "*Stories* make trouble."[21] So they do; that is one reason we need them.

As Matt Wolf says in his review of the London National Theater Production of *Haroun,* "we suppress stories at great cost to ourselves, as Rushdie of all people well knows. Inasmuch as we are the stories we tell, any attempt to close those stories off itself constitutes a murder, . . ."[22]

It is Salman Rushdie's good fortune, ours, and our children's that in spite of everything he has not been silenced. He has survived the death threats of his own Khattam-Shud, and the Sea of Stories from which he drew this entertaining and moving book has not been poisoned, but continues to flow as clear and brilliant as ever.

THE PERILS OF HARRY POTTER

Like many famous children's authors, J. K. (Joanne) Rowling, author of the brilliant and phenomenally successful Harry Potter books, remains in close touch with her own childhood. "I really can, with no difficulty at all, think myself back to 11 years old," she has told *Time* magazine.[1] Rowling is also clearly on the side of children. She has created a world in which her young hero and his friends have special abilities, while conventional adults are either clueless or cruel or both. Her heroes' secret power takes traditional folktale forms (flying brooms, ghosts, transformation, speaking animals, spells, and potions). But it can also be seen as a metaphor for the special powers of childhood: imagination, creativity, and especially humor—as well as being exciting, her books are often very funny.

The Harry Potter stories belong to an ongoing tradition of Anglo American fantasy that begins with Tolkien and T. H. White, and has been continued splendidly by writers like Lloyd Alexander, Susan Cooper, Alan Garner, Patrick Pullman, and Diana Wynne Jones. (Jones's excellent *Charmed Life,* like the Pot-

ter books, takes place in a school for juvenile witches and wizards located in an enchanted castle.) What sets Rowling's books
apart from their predecessors is partly a lighthearted fertility of
invention that recalls L. Frank Baum's Oz books. Even more important is the fact that hers, like Baum's, is a fully imagined
world, to which she has a deep, ongoing commitment. For six
years, even before she began the first book in the series, Rowling was imagining and elaborating its fantasy universe. She has
already planned seven Harry Potter novels, one for each year
Harry will spend at Hogwarts School of Witchcraft and Wizardry, an institution that seems to be located (like J. K. Rowling
herself) somewhere in Scotland.

Harry, Rowling's hero, is a natural-born wizard, but at first
he doesn't know it. When we meet him he is ten years old and
in the classic Cinderlad situation: a poor, lonely orphan, de-
spised and abused. Harry lives with his deeply unpleasant aunt
and uncle, Mr. and Mrs. Dursley, in a country that much resembles Britain in the 1960s or 1970s, before the Internet, digital
phones, and interactive video.

The Dursleys live in a village called Little Whinging (a joke
that American readers may not get: we would call such a place
Little Whining) and, like most of their neighbors, are Muggles—
people who have no magic powers. They hate the very mention
of the supernatural, and refuse to give Harry any information
about his dead parents. ("They were weirdos, no denying it, and
the world's better off without them in my opinion," Uncle Vernon declares.)[2] Uncle Vernon and Aunt Petunia are as cruel to
Harry as any fairy-tale stepparent: they feed him poorly and
clothe him shabbily; they make him sleep in a dark, spider-
infested cupboard under the stairs; and they destroy his mail.
Even worse is their son, Dudley, a spoiled, overweight, greedy
bully who, with the help of his large and hateful friends, makes
Harry's school and home life actively miserable.

From the point of view of an imaginative child, the world is full of Muggles: people who don't understand you, make stupid rules, and want nothing to do with the unexpected or the unseen. Harry's story also embodies the common childhood fantasy that the dreary adults and siblings you live with are not your real family; that you have more exciting parents, and are somehow special and gifted. Harry has an outward manifestation of his gift: a scar in the shape of a lightning bolt on his forehead, the sign that even as a baby he could not be killed by the evil offstage Dark Wizard Voldemort, whose very name most people fear to utter.

As in many folktales, you can often tell a character's character from his or her name, and "Voldemort" neatly combines the ideas of theft, mold, and death. Harry Potter, on the other hand, has a name that suggests not only craftsmanship but both English literature—Shakespeare's Prince Hal and Harry Hotspur, the brave, charming, impulsive heroes of *Henry IV*—and Beatrix Potter, who created that other charming and impulsive classic hero, Peter Rabbit.

At the start of each story Harry Potter is living in exile at the Dursleys'. But presently, with the help of magic, he is rescued and enters an alternate world in which imagination and adventurousness are rewarded. A comic cockney giant named Hagrid introduces him to a parallel magical Britain, one entrance to which is through the back door of a scruffy London pub called The Leaky Cauldron. After a shopping trip in which Harry visits a bank run by goblins and purchases unusual school supplies, including "one plain pointed hat (black) for day wear"[3] and the *Standard Book of Spells* (Grade 1), he takes a special train to the Hogwarts School of Witchcraft and Wizardry from Track Nine and Three-Quarters at King's Cross Station—a train and track that are invisible to Muggles.

Hogwarts School, it turns out, is located in a huge ancient castle, well equipped with towers, dungeons, ghosts, secret passages, and enchanted paintings and mirrors. The subjects taught there include Divination, Defense Against the Dark Arts, and Care of Magical Creatures. But in other ways Hogwarts resembles a classic English boarding school—one that, in keeping with the times, is coed and multiracial. There are four houses, which compete intensely in the school sport of Quidditch, a sort of combination cricket, soccer, and hockey played on flying broomsticks, in which Harry turns out to excel. The teachers wear black gowns and dine at a head table, and there are prefects and a Head Boy and a Head Girl.

Just as in many American schools, however, the student population is roughly divided into jocks, brains, nice guys, and dangerous Goths. Harry and his two best friends are in the jock house, Gryffindor, where, according to tradition, "dwell the brave at heart." Ravenclaw House emphasizes "wit and learning," while the kids in Hufflepuff are described as "just and loyal . . . And unafraid of toil." The bad characters live in Slytherin House, where they "use any means / to achieve their ends."[4]

Even before he arrives at Hogwarts, Harry acquires an enemy in Slytherin House, the mean, snobbish, unscrupulous Draco Malfoy, whose name translates readily into "Dragon Bad-Faith." Like Cousin Dudley in the Muggle world, Draco has a couple of goons (these are named Crabbe and Goyle) to back up his constant sneering and bullying. As a hero and local sports star, Harry also attracts fans; naturally modest, he finds their intense admiration and constant attention as embarrassing as J. K. Rowling reportedly does.

But Harry has more serious problems. The plot of each book essentially centers on the attempts of dark forces to destroy him. As is customary in modern fantasies, from Tolkien's *Lord of the Rings* to *Star Wars,* lurking in the background is an evil, powerful figure (almost always male) who wants to rule the world.[5] Often these characters have something in common with Milton's rebel angels: at first they seem impressive and even glamorous. There is something admirable in their desire for knowledge and power, whereas their followers, motivated mainly by fear, greed, and revenge, are wholly repulsive.

Harry, of course, always escapes his enemies, but this gets harder with each book. Rowling has said that as time passes the stories will turn darker. "There will be deaths," she has informed *Time* magazine.[6] Already in volumes 3 and 4 it is not so easy to tell which side anyone is on. Characters who at first seem friends may be foes, or vice versa; and good but weak people may be seduced into doing evil because of their own fear or folly. In the third volume, *Harry Potter and the Prisoner of Azkaban,* for instance, a scruffy but harmless-looking pet rat called Scabbers turns out to be a wicked wizard who, even in human form, has a pointed nose and small, watery eyes.

Rowling describes her characters with a psychological subtlety rare in children's books and even in much adult fiction. In *Harry Potter and the Chamber of Secrets* a ragged, oppressed house-elf named Dobby is constantly torn between loyalty to his evil masters and his wish to save Harry's life. Whenever he is on the edge of revealing their plots, Dobby hits himself over the head with the nearest blunt object, repeating "Bad Dobby!"

Another attraction of the Potter books is that the good characters are not perfect. Harry excels at Quidditch, but he is only an average student, unlike his friend Hermione, who studies for the fun of it and is a bit of a prig. Hagrid, the lovable giant gamekeeper, has a weakness for dangerous magic creatures: he sees his vicious pet dragon and the huge spiders that live in the Forbidden Forest as cute and cuddly. The British, of course, are fanatic animal-lovers; and it may be that this is Rowling's comment on the peculiar or even dangerous but beloved pets that visitors to England sometimes encounter.

Though Rowling's child heroes are imperfect, they are usually smarter and braver than adults. Some of the nicest teachers at Hogwarts, though friendly and knowledgeable, often don't have a clue as to what's going on around them. Others are weak and incompetent, or complete phonies like the handsome media-intoxicated Professor Lockhart, who claims to have performed the magical exploits of other, less photogenic wizards. A few have even sold out to the Dark Powers or their representatives.

The headmaster of Hogwarts, the elderly silver-haired Professor Dumbledore (like Tolkien's Gandalf, whom he much resembles), maintains a kind of benign detachment from events except in moments of great crisis. A. O. Scott, writing in the on-line magazine *Slate,* has perceptively remarked that "Dumbledore's benevolent but strict theology, involving the operations of free will in a supernaturally determined world, is classically Miltonian."[7]

The appeal of the Harry Potter books, to judge by the flood of reviews and essays that greeted their appearance, is wide and varied. They can be enjoyed, for instance, as the celebration of a preindustrial world: Hogwarts Castle is lit by torches and heated by fires, and mail is carried by owls of different sizes, including tiny little scops owls ("Local Deliveries Only"). As with most first-rate children's books, there is something here for everyone. Pico Iyer, in *The New York Times Book Review,* sees the stories as only half-fantastic accounts of life in an English public school (in his case, Eton), "designed to train the elite in a system that other mortals cannot follow." There, as at Hogwarts, he claims, "we were in an alternative reality where none of the usual rules applied."[8] A. O. Scott, on the other hand, thinks that "being a wizard is very much like being gay: you grow up in a hostile world governed by codes and norms that seem nonsensical to you, and you discover at a certain age that there are people like you."[9] (It seems unlikely that Harry Potter is gay; in the third volume he shows romantic interest in an extremely pretty Quidditch player called Cho Chang, and in volume 4 he proudly takes a student called Parvati Patil to the Yule Ball.)

*

Any wildly successful work of art attracts detractors as well as admirers of all sorts. The most famous liberal scholar of the folktale, Jack Zipes, has called the books overrated, and criticized them for promoting a conventional, patriarchal view of the world.[10] On the other hand, in the American South and Midwest, and in Southern California, the sort of conservatives who object to the teaching of evolution and the big bang theory of creation have complained that the stories portray witchcraft in a favorable light. This is not a new idea: from time to time the same accusation has been made against the Oz books, which in some cases have then been removed from schools and libraries along with all other representations of cute or friendly wizards and witches.

In my favorite local bookshop the other day, I saw what at first seemed to be two new Harry Potter books displayed on the counter. One was called *Pokemon and Harry Potter*, the other *Harry Potter and the Bible*. But instead of additions to the series, they turned out to be warnings. In the first, by Phil Arms, I read that "the dark occultic nature of Harry Potter . . . is opening the lives and homes of countless millions of parents and children to satanic influences."[11] The second went even further, suggesting that "an unseen spiritual force of darkness"[12] may be driving the Potter phenomenon.

According to Richard Abanes, the author of *Harry Potter and the Bible*, "the Harry Potter series is not morally compatible with Christianity."[13] The books are "filled with potentially harmful messages exalting occultism and moral relativism."[14] Abanes is dismayed by the many parallels between the authors of the magical textbooks Harry studies and the names of historical occultists, and hints that J. K. Rowling may be more involved in contemporary witchcraft than she admits. He speaks of "the very tangible possibility that many children will become so enthralled with magic and wizardry that they will seek out the paganism/witchcraft that is available in the real world."[15]

Abanes also complains that Harry Potter and his friends are not model children. They break rules, disobey orders, and sometimes conceal their rebellious behavior by lying. Moreover, "they are often rather proud of themselves and their misdeeds."[16] The books contain what he calls "countless examples of behavior that Christian parents would deem less than admirable, not to mention unbiblical."[17] This is quite true, and is probably one of the reasons for Harry Potter's popularity with kids; it is also in the great tradition of children's literature. Tom Sawyer and his friends drink, smoke tobacco, swear, and play truant from school. In *The Wizard of Oz* Dorothy refuses to do housework for the Wicked Witch of the West, and Mary Lennox in *The Secret Garden* disobeys and deceives adults, finding her way not only into the forbidden garden but into the room of her invalid cousin Colin, whose existence has been concealed from her. Books like these do not present their child characters as perfect and obedient, but as curious, independent, and enterprising.

As an antidote to Harry Potter, Richard Abanes proposes the works of Tolkien and especially C. S. Lewis. If the antidote is to be effective, however, it may have to be taken soon: a recent article in *The New York Times* announced that "the Lewis estate and its publishers have started shaping a marketing makeover." They have "developed a discreet strategy to avoid direct links to the Christian imagery and theology that suffused the Narnia novels and inspired Lewis."[18]

Anyone who is familiar with the works of C. S. Lewis will realize that it will be almost impossible to take Christianity out of Narnia. Lewis's books are consciously founded on Christian theology; there is a witch in the series, but as Abanes says, "She is evil and based on age-old and widely accepted symbols and illustrations of evil."[19] In the world of Narnia, virtue consists in loving and serving the great lion Aslan, a Christ-like figure who in *The Lion, the Witch, and the Wardrobe* sacrifices himself to redeem the child Edmund from moral enslavement to the witch.

In Narnia, final happiness is the result not of individual initiative and enterprise, but of submission to the wisdom and will of superior beings. Misbehavior can be forgiven if it is sincerely repented, and Edmund eventually becomes one of the Kings of Narnia. His older sister, Susan, however, loses her title at the end of the series because "she's interested in nothing nowadays except nylons and lipstick and invitations."[20]

One complaint that both Abanes and Arms make against the Potter books is that in them evil and good are ambiguous and shifting. Apparently harmless or innocent characters turn out to be working for dark forces, and wicked-looking characters are revealed to be messengers of light. In Narnia, on the other hand, good and evil are clearly distinguishable. The good supernatural figures often come from classical mythology, the bad ones from European folklore. In the battle at the end of *The Lion, the Witch, and the Wardrobe,* Aslan is supported by good giants and unicorns and centaurs and fauns; the Witch by an army of ogres and wolves and apes and hags and wraiths.

The world of Narnia is simple and eternal: goodness, peace, and beauty will eventually triumph. The world of Harry Potter is complex and ambiguous and fluid. And in this, of course, it is far more like our own world, in which it is not always easy to tell the ogres from the giants. When we choose books for our children, do we want them to teach obedience to authority or skepticism, acceptance of the status quo or a determination to change what needs to be changed?

Joanne Rowling's own story, like Harry's, is in the classic European folklore tradition. As almost everyone now knows, when she was working on *Harry Potter and the Sorcerer's Stone*,[21] she was a young single mother with long red hair, living on public assistance in Edinburgh. Because her flat was unheated, she would put her small daughter into a stroller and push her about the streets until the child fell asleep. Then she would go to a cafe, order a cup of coffee, and write.

Rowling's fairy godmother was the Scottish Arts Council, which gave her a grant that made it possible for her to finish the first volume. But even then she had trouble getting transportation to the ball. Nine English publishers rejected *Harry Potter and the Philosopher's Stone* before Bloomsbury took it, and her editors had no idea it would be a success. At first they made no special attempt to promote the book, and printed only a small number of copies.

Now, of course, all that is history. At one point the first three volumes of the series were number one, two, and three on *The New York Times* best-seller list. This annoyed publishers of adult fiction so much, and their protests were so vociferous, that the editors of the paper finally agreed to begin listing juvenile best-sellers separately. The first volume has been translated into (at last count) twenty-eight languages. A plain-cover edition has also appeared in England, for adults who are embarrassed to be seen reading a children's book. Though this edition costs two pounds more than the original, it very soon sold twenty thousand copies.

In the fall of 2001 the Warner Brothers film of *Harry Potter and the Sorcerer's Stone* opened to generally good reviews and crowds of fans. To accompany the release there were Harry Potter T-shirts, lunch boxes, video games, and action figures. There were also even more interviews with J. K. Rowling, and more intrusive articles about her life.

For Rowling herself this was clearly not an unmixed blessing. In the fourth volume of the series, *Harry Potter and the Goblet of Fire*, Harry is persecuted by the repellent Rita Skeeter, a scandal-sniffing female reporter for the tabloid *Daily Prophet*, who does her best to persuade Harry's friends to betray his secrets, and nearly causes a disaster.

Whatever she feels about all this attention and success, the folktale heroine J. K. Rowling, once a welfare mother, has clearly now become a fabulously rich princess. Will she now find true love and live happily ever after? Will she be destroyed by the curses of fundamentalist Christians, or fall under the spell of wicked merchandisers and publicists? Her story promises to be almost as interesting as the future adventures of Harry Potter himself.

WHAT FAIRY TALES TELL US

T HE stories of magic and transformation that we call "fairy tales" (though they usually contain no fairies) are one of the oldest known forms of literature, and also one of the most popular and enduring. Even today they are a central part of our imaginative world. We remember and refer to them all our lives; their themes and characters reappear in dreams, in songs, in films, in advertisements, and in casual speech. We say that someone is a giant-killer or that theirs is a Cinderella story.

The fairy tale survives because it presents experience in vivid symbolic form. Sometimes we need to have the truth exaggerated and made more dramatic, even fantastic, in order to comprehend it. (The same sort of thing can occur in other ways, of course, as when at a costume party we suddenly recognize that one of our acquaintances is in fact essentially a six-foot-tall white rabbit, a pirate, or a dancing doll.)

"Hansel and Gretel," for instance, may dramatize the fact that some parents underfeed and neglect their children physically and/or emotionally, while others, like the witch who lives in a house made of cake and candy, overfeed and try to possess and perhaps even devour them. "Beauty and the Beast" may suggest that a good man can seem at first like a dangerous wild animal, or that true love has a power to soothe the savage heart. The message may be different for each reader; that is one of the great achievements of the fairy tale, traditional or modern.

For though not everyone knows it, there are modern fairy tales. Though most people think of these stories as having come into existence almost magically long ago, they are in fact still being created, and not only in less urbanized parts of the world than our own. Over the last century and a half many famous authors have written tales of wonder and enchantment. In Britain and America they have included Nathaniel Hawthorne, Charles Dickens, Robert Louis Stevenson, Oscar Wilde, H. G. Wells, Carl Sandburg, James Thurber, Bernard Malamud, I. B. Singer, T. H. White, Angela Carter, and Louise Erdrich. Like other authors in other countries (especially France and Germany) they have used the characters and settings and events of the fairy tale to create new and marvelous stories—not only for children, but for adults. The traditional fairy tale was not read from a book but passed on orally from one generation to the next, and its audience was not limited to children. Its heroes and heroines most often are not children but young people setting out to make their fortunes or find a mate, or most often both. Many of these stories were written for readers of all ages, or only for adults. But even when they were principally meant for children, and have child protagonists, these modern tales often contain sophisticated comments and ironic asides directed to the adults who might be reading the story aloud.

The best modern fairy stories, like traditional folktales, can be understood in many different ways. Like all great literature, they speak to readers of every place and time. They have one message for a seven-year-old and another one, more complex and sometimes more melancholy, for a seventeen-year-old or a seventy-year-old; they may mean one thing to a nineteenth-century reader and another to a twentieth-century one.

George MacDonald's "The Light Princess" (1864), for example, is on the face of it a traditional tale of enchantment. When the princess is born, her parents, in the time-honored manner, fail to invite a wicked witch (who is also the king's sister) to the christening party. As a result, the witch curses the baby with a lack of gravity. This lack manifests itself both physically and psychologically: the princess weighs nothing, and she also is incapable of serious emotions; in contemporary parlance, she is a total airhead. Eventually a prince falls in love with the Light Princess. He is willing to sacrifice his life for her, and when the princess finally realizes it, she too falls in love, and this breaks the enchantment. The prince is restored to life, and they are married and live happily ever after.

A modern reader might come away from this story thinking it says that the best way to grow up fast is to fall in love. To a Victorian reader, however, it would more likely have seemed to be about the proper behavior of women. At the time it was generally considered, as the Light Princess's Queen remarks, a bad thing for a woman to be light-headed and light-minded. Later on the prince who loves her is pleased to discover that when the princess swims in the lake, she is "not so forward in her questions, or pert in her replies. . . . Neither did she laugh so much, and when she did laugh, it was more gently. She seemed altogether more modest and maidenly."[1] Like the ideal Victorian girl, the princess becomes gentle, quiet, and above all serious.

The earliest attempts to create modern fairy tales were tentative. At first, authors merely rewrote the traditional stories of Grimm and Perrault, sometimes in what now seems a ridiculous manner. In 1853 the Grimms' first English illustrator, George Cruickshank, began to publish revisions of the most popular tales from a teetotal point of view. The Giant in his "Jack and the Beanstalk" turns out to be an alcoholic, and Cinderella's wedding is celebrated by the destruction of all the drink in the Prince's castle.

Meanwhile, other writers were beginning to go beyond revision to compose original tales, often in order to point out an improving moral. The lesson, of course, varied with the convictions of the author. Catherine Sinclair's lighthearted "Uncle David's Nonsensical Story About Giants and Fairies" (1839) suggested that idle and overfed children were apt to be eaten alive, while Juliana Horatia Ewing's "Good Luck Is Better Than Gold" (1882) and Howard Pyle's "The Apple of Contentment" (1886) punished greed and laziness.

Some writers were concerned with more contemporary issues. John Ruskin's famous ecological fable, "The King of the Golden River" (1851), promotes both his political and his aesthetic beliefs. The two wicked older brothers in this story are shortsighted capitalists who exploit both labor and natural resources, turning a once-fertile and dramatically beautiful valley into a barren wasteland. Their moods are so dark and their hearts so hard that it seems quite appropriate that they should eventually be transformed into two black stones, while little Gluck, who appreciates the sublime natural landscape and relieves the sufferings of the poor and disabled, restores the land to beauty and fruitfulness.

In "A Toy Princess" (1877) Mary De Morgan mounts a scathing attack on the ideal Victorian miss. The courtiers among whom her heroine grows up scold her for expressing her feelings, and much prefer the artificial doll-princess who never says anything but "If you please," "No thank you," "Certainly," and "Just so."[2] With the help of a good fairy, the real princess escapes from the palace and finds happiness and love in a fisherman's family.

More unsettling, and with a darker ending, is Lucy Lane Clifford's "The New Mother" (1882), which tells of the awful fate of two innocent children who are repeatedly encouraged in naughty behavior by a strange and charming young woman who may be an evil spirit. Eventually the children try their mother's patience so far that she threatens to leave them and send home a new mother, with glass eyes and a wooden tail. Anyone who has ever seen a harassed parent appear to turn temporarily into a glassy-eyed monster—or done so themselves—will understand this story instinctively, and so will parents who have doubts about the moral qualities of their baby-sitters. The author was a good friend of Henry James, and it is possible that "The New Mother" may be one of the sources of *The Turn of the Screw*.

After Perrault and Grimm the greatest influence on the literary fairy tale was Hans Christian Andersen, whose work was first translated into English in 1846. Andersen's early tales were adaptations of those he had heard from his grandmother, with their commonsense pagan fatality overlaid with Christian morality; later he composed original stories that often celebrated the nineteenth-century virtues of stoicism, piety, and self-sacrifice.

Andersen's romantic, spiritual narratives were echoed in the work of Oscar Wilde and Laurence Housman, among many others. Often their tales seem remarkably modern. In Housman's "The Rooted Lover" (1894) the hero is what my students at Cornell would call a postfeminist man. Like the prince in George MacDonald's "The Light Princess," he does not fight giants and dragons, but shows his courage and virtue through patient endurance for the sake of love.

In Wilde's "The Selfish Giant" (1888) Christian morality and myth dominate. The traditional fairy-tale villain of the title is not slain but reformed by a child who turns out to be Christ. Other writers, following Andersen's example, abandoned the usual happy ending of the fairy tale to create stories with an ambiguous or disturbing conclusion, like Robert Louis Stevenson's "The Song of the Morrow" (1894) in which a series of events is endlessly repeated in an almost Kafka-like manner.

Not all nineteenth-century British fairy tales are this serious:

many are quietly or broadly comic. There are good-natured burlesques like Charles Dickens's "The Magic Fishbone" (1868) in which a scatty Micawber-like (or Dickens-like) family is saved by the patience and good sense of the eldest daughter; and there are gentle satires of social conformity and cowardice, like Frances Browne's "The Story of Fairyfoot" (1856), which exposes the arbitrary nature of standards of beauty, imagining a kingdom where the larger your feet are, the better-looking you are thought to be. Perhaps the best known of such stories is Kenneth Grahame's "The Reluctant Dragon" (1898), possibly the first overtly pacifist fairy tale. It features a sentimental dragon who writes sonnets and only wishes to be admired by the villagers whom he has terrified; many readers will recognize a common human type.

The fashion for tales that were humorous and satirical as well as (or instead of) uplifting or improving continued into the early twentieth century. E. Nesbit's "The Book of Beasts" (1900) is a lighthearted fable about the magical power of art. The volume that contains this title has pictures of exotic creatures that come alive when the pages are opened. The boy who finds the book releases first a butterfly, then a Blue Bird of Paradise, and finally a dragon that threatens to destroy the country. If any book is vivid enough, this story seems to say, its content will invade our world for good or evil.

For H. G. Wells, magic was allied with, or a metaphor for, science. His rather spooky Magic Shop, in the story of the same name (1903), contains both traditional supernatural creatures, like a small angry red demon, and the actual inventions of the future, including a train that runs without steam.

Other twentieth-century British writers composed more romantic tales. Some, like Walter de la Mare's "The Lovely Myfawny" (1925) and Sylvia Townsend Warner's witty "Bluebeard's Daughter" (1940), have a traditional fairy-story background of castles and princesses, and rebuke old-fashioned faults—in the former case, possessive paternal love; in the latter, curiosity.

Others are set in the contemporary world. John Collier's "The Chaser" (1941), a very short story with a sting in its tale, takes place in modern London; Naomi Mitchison's "In the Family" (1957) is set in a Scotland complete with buses and parish halls— and a fairy woman who warns the hero of a future highway accident.

Often these twentieth-century tales are interesting variations on earlier classics. Lord Dunsany's "The Kith of the Elf-Folk" (1910) is a half-poetic, half-satirical version of Andersen's "The Little Mermaid," with a happier, though rather conservative conclusion. In it a Wild Thing from the marshes ends by rejecting both her newly acquired human soul and a singing career in London. She returns to her former life and companions in the depths of the countryside—as other strange wild young women have sometimes done.

More recently the gifted British writer Angela Carter has become famous for her dramatic retellings of well-known fairy tales. Though her stories are as full of mystery and wonder, they are clearly set in modern times: Bluebeard's castle is connected to Paris by telephone, and in "The Courtship of Mr. Lyon" (1979) Beauty returns to her dying Beast from contemporary London on a train. Her characters too have been subtly updated: her Beast is Mr. Lyon, the awkward, lonely, growling owner of a Palladian villa equipped with politely rather than magically invisible servants. Beauty temporarily abandons Mr. Lyon to become a spoiled urban society girl who "smiled at herself in mirrors a little too often,"[3] but later she as well as he is transformed by the power of love. In another version of the same story, "The Tiger's Bride," the hero does not become a handsome prince; instead Beauty is transformed into a tigress by his passionate kisses. The implication is that the magical world is not a thing of the past but may coexist with ours. Perhaps, at any moment, we may enter it.

Some modern British authors of fairy tales, like these, revel in descriptions of exotic or luxurious settings. Others, by contrast, sometimes seem deliberately to choose the drabbest and most ordinary backgrounds, as if to remind us that strange and wonderful things can happen anywhere. Joan Aiken's "The Man Who Had Seen the Rope Trick" (1976) takes place in a dreary English seaside boardinghouse, and T. H. White, in "The Troll" (1935), begins with a similarly pedestrian setting, a comfortable railway hotel in northern Sweden where his hero has gone for the fishing. During his first night there he discovers that the professor in the next room is a troll who has eaten his wife. We accept this, and all that follows, not only because of White's great literary skill but because we know that some men, even some professors, are really trolls, and that some husbands do, psychologically at least, devour their wives (and wives their husbands).

In the nineteenth century it was sometimes suggested that Americans didn't need fairy tales, certainly not new ones. Instead of imaginary wonders we had the natural wonders of a new continent: we had Indians and wild animals instead of sprites and dragons; Niagara Falls and the Rockies instead of enchanted lakes and mountains.

However, Americans were already writing new fairy tales. Sometimes these stories featured old-fashioned props and characters: magic potions and spells, dwarves and witches, princes and princesses. But often they also included contemporary objects and figures: hotels and telephones, mayors and gold miners. And even from the beginning the best American stories had a different underlying message than many of those from across the Atlantic.

The standard European fairy tale, both traditional and modern, takes place in a fixed social world. In the usual plot a poor boy or girl, through some combination of luck, courage, beauty, kindness, and supernatural help, becomes rich or marries into royalty. In a variation, a prince or princess who has fallen under an evil enchantment, or been cast out by a cruel relative, regains his or her rightful position. These stories are full of wicked step-mothers and cruel kings and queens, but they seldom attack the institutions of marriage or monarchy. It is assumed that what the heroine or hero wants is to become rich and marry well. Usually the social system is implicitly unquestioned, and remains un-changed; what changes is the protagonist, and what he or she hopes for is to succeed within the terms of this system.

What makes American fairy tales different is that in many of them this does not happen. Instead, the world within the story alters, or is abandoned. In Washington Irving's "Rip Van Winkle" (1820) Rip falls into a twenty-year sleep and wakes to find that a British colony has become a new nation, in which "the very character of the people seemed changed."[4]

Even if the world does not change, its values are often im-plicitly criticized. The guests who visit "The Rich Man's Place" (1880) in Horace Scudder's story of that name enjoy the palatial house and grounds but don't express any desire to live there. In Frank Stockton's "The Bee-Man of Orn" (1887) a Junior Sorcerer discovers that an old beekeeper has been transformed from his original shape, and sets out to dissolve the enchantment. But as it turns out his original shape (like everyone's) was that of a baby. The Junior Sorcerer restores him to infancy, but when he grows up he does not become a prince, but a beekeeper again—and as before he is perfectly contented.

In American fairy tales there is often not much to be said for wealth and high position, or even for good looks. In Nathaniel Hawthorne's "Feathertop" (1854) a New England witch trans-forms an old scarecrow into a fine gentleman and sends him out into the world, where he exposes the superficiality and snob-bery of the well-to-do. In some ways the story is a democratic version of Mary De Morgan's "A Toy Princess." The scarecrow's

vocabulary, like that of the Toy Princess, is very limited, consisting only of phrases like "Really! Indeed! Pray tell me! Is it
possible! Upon my word! By no means! O! Ah!" and "Hem,"[5] but
he is taken by the local people for a foreign nobleman and almost succeeds in winning the heart and hand of a good and
beautiful girl. Though both these stories end without any real
damage having been done, they are full of the unease we feel
in the presence of someone with fine clothes and impenetrably
bland good manners.

L. Frank Baum's "The Queen of Quok" (1901) contains a castle and royal personages, but Quok is essentially ruled by common sense and small-town American values. At one point the
boy king has to borrow a dime from his chief counselor to buy
a ham sandwich. Love of money turns the would-be queen into
a haggard old woman, while the insouciant young hero lives
happily ever after. And in Baum's "The Glass Dog" (1901) the
poor glassblower manages to marry a princess, but she "was
very jealous of his beauty and led him a dog's life."[6] The implication of such stories is that an American does not need to become rich or marry up in order to be happy; in fact, one should
avoid doing so if possible. Happiness is all around one already,
as the boy in Laura Richards's story "The Golden Window"
(c. 1904) discovers: his farmhouse already has "windows of gold
and diamond" when the setting sun shines on it.

Even further from the traditional pattern are Carl Sandburg's
Rootabaga Stories (1922), which reflect his love of American tall
tales and deadpan humor, as well as his closeness to his pioneer
ancestors. The family in his "How They Broke Away to Go to the
Rootabaga Country" repeats the experience of many nineteenth-
century immigrants to the Midwest. They sell all their possessions and ride to "where the railroad tracks run off into the sky,"[7]
ending up not in a fairy kingdom but in rich farming country
named after a large turnip. "The Story of Blixie Bimber and the
Power of the Gold Buckskin Whincher" takes place in what is

obviously the early-twentieth-century Midwest, complete with hayrides, band concerts, and steeplejacks. But magic is still potent, and romantic passion is a kind of inexplicable spell. "The first man you meet with an X in his name you must fall head over heels in love with him, said the silent power in the gold buckskin whincher,"[8] and Blixie Bimber does, the traditional three times.

Other American fairy tales also take place in a contemporary, unromantic milieu. In Philip K. Dick's "The King of the Elves" (1953), for instance, the future leader of the elves turns out to be an old man in charge of a rundown rural gas station. Anyone, the story says, no matter how mundane his circumstances, may be a magical hero in disguise.

Sometimes American authors used the stock figures of the folktale to criticize contemporary skepticism: James Thurber's famous comic fable "The Unicorn in the Garden" (1949) presents the triumph of a mild visionary over his would-be oppressors: the police, a psychiatrist, and a hostile, suspicious wife who thinks that anyone who sees unicorns is mad.

Some modern American writers have taken the conventions of the folktale or children's story and turned them upside down, as real life sometimes does. In Richard Kennedy's "The Porcelain Man" (1987) the heroine declines to rescue the enchanted hero, whose only attractive quality is his beauty. Another strange reversal occurs in Ursula Le Guin's "The Wife's Story" (1982), a werewolf tale related by a wolf, which can be read as a brief but terrifying fable about family love, madness, and social prejudice.

Many of the best recent American fairy tales comment on twentieth-century events. In Bernard Malamud's "The Jewbird" (1963) a talking crow flies into the Lower East Side apartment of a frozen-foods salesman and announces that he is fleeing from anti-Semites. To judge by what happens next, he may be one of those immigrant survivors of the Holocaust whom some American Jews, after the Second World War, found burdensome. Donald Bartheleme's experimental "The Glass Mountain" (1970) takes off from a traditional story of the same name in Andrew Lang's *The Yellow Fairy Book*, and manages simultaneously to expose the callous ambition of New Yorkers and the formulaic analysis of literary scholars. The mountain he climbs is a skyscraper, and he rejects the princess because she is only "an enchanted symbol." In the late twentieth century American writers also began to compose tales of magic based upon previously untapped folk traditions. Many of Isaac Bashevis Singer's stories, including "Menaseh's Dream" (1968), draw on Jewish folk beliefs and make wise, if disguised, comments on Jewish life, in this case on the power of memory and of family love. Louise Erdrich, in "Old Man Potchikoo" (1989), uses the Native American trickster tale as a starting point for celebration of Dionysian energy.

Several writers, both British and American, have produced fairy tales with a strong feminist slant. Among them are Tanith Lee's "Prince Amilec" (1972), Jay Williams's "Petronella" (1973), and Jeanne Desy's inventive "The Princess Who Stood on Her Own Two Feet" (1982), in which a well-meaning young woman gives up more and more of her natural abilities in order to make her fiancé feel good about himself—a procedure that unfortunately may still be observed in real life. In the end, of course, she rebels and refuses to marry the prince. And in Angela Carter's "Bluebeard" (1979) the heroine is rescued not by her brothers but by her mother, who has already killed a man-eating tiger.

Another interesting example of the genre is Jane Yolen's "The River Maid" (1982). The protagonists of Yolen's poetic fairy tales are often prefeminist: delicate, passive, and either victimized or self-sacrificing or both. But in "The River Maid," though the eponymous heroine remains frail and helpless, the river of which she is the guardian spirit is strong. A greedy farmer dams and diverts the water to enrich his fields, and abducts and rapes the River Maid. The following spring the river rises, washes away the farm, and drowns the farmer. Afterward it can be heard "playing merrily over [his] bones," with a "high, sweet, bubbling song . . . full of freedom and a conquering joy."[9] Women may be imprisoned and abused, the story seems to say, but time and the forces of nature will avenge them.

Today, the fairy tale is often dismissed as old-fashioned, sentimental, and silly: a minor form of literature, appropriate only for children. To readers who have been overexposed to the bowdlerized and prettified cartoon versions of the classic stories, this criticism may seem justified. But any reader who knows the authentic traditional tales, or the many brilliant modern variations on their themes, will realize that fairy tales are not merely childish entertainments set in an unreal and irrelevant universe. Though they can and do entertain children, we will do well to listen seriously to what they tell us about the real world we live in.

BOYS AND GIRLS COME OUT
TO PLAY: CHILDREN'S GAMES

Mᴏsᴛ readers of this book, though they may have enjoyed childhood, were not totally happy in elementary school. I am reminded of this when I see boys and girls waiting for the yellow bus on a misty autumn morning. They look serious, tensed up, uncertain of what lies ahead. They know that even if events in the classroom are predictable, recess will be an interlude of near anarchy in which anything can happen. They may be admired or mocked, attacked or welcomed, know sudden triumph or crushing humiliation.

As the British folklorist Iona Opie puts it in *The People in the Playgound,* childhood "is a time more full of fears and anxieties than many adults care to remember."[1] Few of us revisit elementary school as we do secondary school and college. The idea that someone might deliberately return to this scene and spend months and even years hanging about, without the pay and official status of a teacher, seems odd.

Yet Iona Opie herself in England, and Barrie Thorne in America, did just that during roughly the same period—the late

1970s—with interesting results. They also witnessed many of the same phenomena; but their stance as observers, the manner in which they report their discoveries, and the works that resulted, are wholly different. Iona Opie's attitude toward the children whose activities she recorded is one of affectionate sympathy, and though she makes few attempts to analyze the rich original material she has collected, her journal is a pleasure to read. She writes in the British tradition of the amateur naturalist and essayist, assuming a wide but literate audience who will understand references to Rabelais or Rossetti. Barrie Thorne, who was far less comfortable on the playground, is a professor writing for professors, which traditionally requires a more formal manner. Her *Gender Play* is sometimes hard going, but it contains many interesting and original observations.

Iona Opie is now probably the world's best-known authority on the culture of childhood; she shared this honor with her husband, Peter, until his death in 1982. Together the Opies more or less invented the study of juvenile games, rhymes, and songs, publishing now-classic works like *The Oxford Dictionary of Nursery Rhymes, The Lore and Language of Schoolchildren,* and *Children's Games in Street and Playground.* In 1960 Mrs. Opie began to spend time at a state elementary school near her home in Hampshire; between 1970 and 1983 she made regular weekly visits to it. The resulting book, in journal form, is "a narrative account of what one person could see and overhear and be told directly during the fifteen eventful minutes of morning playtime," from January 1970 to July 1980.[2]

Iona Opie seems to have known instinctively how to present herself to children. When she appears they crowd around, jostling for the chance to tell a joke or a rhyme, or draw her into their fantasies. "The bold bad story-teller caught up with me," she writes of one encounter, "brandishing a length of joined elastic bands and saying, 'This is a threatening machine.'"[3]

For her, the experience was exhilarating. Even after twenty

years of observation, she writes, "I still feel the excitement of the hunter when I hear children coming out to play."[4] The playground is a thrilling place where "there is always something to copy, something to watch, something to join in."[5] She admires the children's imagination, the way they can instantly throw themselves into a fantasy. "'We're playing Anti-tanks and Anti-aeroplanes . . . killing elephants and the warring mammoths,'" one confides. "'That's how they got extinct.'"[6]

But Iona Opie is by no means sentimental about children. Sometimes she sees them as temporary lunatics or angry savages:

> I stood watching . . . and thought, "Playtime is a chance to go mad." The children were pushing, clutching, staggering, prancing, dodging, exaggerating every moment into pantomime; it was continuous Saturnalia.[7]

She writes of

> the savage noises of the playground: the aggressive and defensive shouting—"Nah, gettaway," "Watch it, you dope,"—and the wordless invective of screams and snarls. Hobbes, I thought, was right in his belief that man is committed to endless conflict.[8]

At other times children appear to her as instinctive humorists:

> Try to analyse the sound of children at play: the thin screaming noise can be heard from several streets away. Vitality? Yes. But come closer and step into the playground; a kind of defiant light heartedness envelops you. The children are . . . making fun of life.[9]

Usually Mrs. Opie describes rather than analyzes; but her range is both broad and detailed. She records the weather and the way people move and speak: "The sky overcast, with glaring white light shining through. House-martins hunted . . . directly overhead."[10] "A maelstrom of wind and small wet snow."[11] "As a boy begins to run away from a chaser his eyes open wider."[12]

Part of the charm of Iona Opie's book is that she often reacts as if she were a child herself. "A boy was standing and writing in the middle of the playground. I felt a sense of kinship, and competition."[13] She identifies the children as a child might: "the mouse boy," "the gorilla boy," "the chorus girl," and "the freckle-faced horror." She describes a hollow in the grass as "a depression deep enough for a platypus to nest in," and takes notes with a pencil she had decorated with silver sealing wax when she was ten. Reporting on an encounter with two little girls, she speaks as if she were exactly their age: "We were quite content to laugh together about nothing in particular (an enjoyment not comprehensible to adults). . . ."[14]

Iona Opie admires the spontaneous and natural and is put off by self-consciousness. She is especially irritated by a girl named Lisa, who appears to be what might be called an unauthentic subject. Lisa, Mrs. Opie remarks, is "a damned nuisance. It is 'Miss, watch this!' all the time. She showed me several boring sequences with a ball today. . . . She invents these things especially for me, so that I will write them down. I am sure she would not play them otherwise."[15]

When the material Mrs. Opie is offered is authentic, nothing bores or shocks her, though at one point she does become weary of the inane washroom jokes offered by two children she calls "the naughty boys." "Perhaps they were possessed," she suggests after they have contributed a characteristic rhyme. ("Hey diddle diddle, The cat done a piddle, The cow done a poo on the floor.")[16] Most of the material Iona Opie is so eagerly offered is harmless or even witty. ("What lies on the bottom of the sea and shivers? A nervous wreck.")[17] She enjoys it even when the joke is on her:

The story-teller . . . was prancing round me, clutching a plastic bag of biscuit crumbs. "You ain't having none of these,"
he chortled. "Oh, where did you get them from?" I asked, for-
getting that he was not a fellow housewife. "Up the common," he said, "when I was digging for food."[18]

As might be expected, *The People in the Playground* is full of
remarkable rhymes and games. Some go back more than a hundred years; others are topical and prove again that it is impossible to shield children from contemporary life:

> One banana, two banana, three banana, four,
> Fifteen skinheads knocking at the door,
> Five with machine guns, five with sticks,
> Five with hand grenades hanging from their—
> la la. la la la . . .[19]

A few are romantic and surrealist:

> Please, Mr. Crocodile, may we cross your golden river
> In a silver boat?
> If not, why not?
> What is your favourite color?[20]

Even if it were magically possible, few children would want to
experience forty consecutive periods of recess. Most readers,
similarly, will not choose to read *The People in the Playground*
straight through, unless they are interested in observing an
ethnographer in action; but you can open it anywhere and find
something to enjoy.

Barrie Thorne's *Gender Play,* on the other hand, is not the
sort of book you can dip into for fun. Part of the problem is its
style: Professor Thorne does not cling to social science jargon;
she wants to lighten up, but doesn't always manage it. Half-dead
metaphors jostle each other uneasily in her prose; as she says in

a sentence that proves its own point, "Different angles of vision lurk within seemingly simple choices of language."[21] Also, though she has much to say about the culture of childhood, Thorne seems to have been less comfortable than Iona Opie at the schools she visited in California and Michigan in 1966–67 and 1980. She began with some disadvantages, of course: she was twenty years younger than Mrs. Opie and far less experienced as an observer of children; and she was trying to do much more. The Opies, as folklorists, assumed that it was enough to collect material. Barrie Thorne believed that a book must have a thesis, a focus of interest. Hers, as her title suggests, was the difference between how boys and girls play at school.

Superficially, Professor Thorne's methods are more detached than those of Iona Opie. She does not spend much time talking to kids, because she is not interested in individual behavior, but in what she calls "group life."[22] But in another sense her approach is far more personal. As she tells us, she is a feminist and the daughter of a feminist, and has been "active in the women's movement."[23] She and her husband (who, like Iona Opie's, is called Peter) are "alert to the forces of gender socialization" and determined "to help our son and daughter break through this kind of channeling."[24]

Barrie Thorne's approach to her subject is conscientious. She begins by consulting the *Oxford English Dictionary* with a magnifying glass to discover the possible meanings of the word *play,* and critically reading many of the studies that have preceded hers. In spite of her focus on groups, she is aware of individual differences and rejects the idea that all members of the same sex are alike. She complains that previous researchers have tended to concentrate on the most "masculine" boys and the most "feminine" girls, ignoring tomboys and sissies, thus exaggerating gender differences. In some cases, she sees *"a skew towards the most visible and dominant,"*[25] and suggests that observers have tended to identify with the most popular kids and neglect to pay attention to the loners. She is also honest enough to see this process occurring in her own fieldwork, and tries to counteract it:

> After a few weeks . . . I realized that my fieldnotes were obsessed with documenting Kathryn's popularity. . . . Then I realized the envy behind my note-taking and analysis and recalled that many years ago when I was a fourth- and fifth-grader of middling social status, I had also carefully watched the popular girl.[26]

She finds the same bias in other researchers. "I detect a kind of yearning in these books," she says of one group of studies, all by men; "when they went back to scenes from their earlier lives, the authors couldn't resist hanging out at the top."[27]

Unlike Iona Opie, Barrie Thorne was ill at ease on the playground. "Several kids asked me if I was a spy, and, in a way, I was, especially when I went in search of the activities and meanings they created when not in the company of adults."[28] She also ran into trouble with her cover story. Mrs. Opie explained herself as someone with "the sensible and interesting hobby of collecting games, rhymes, and jokes,"[29] a hobby that children, who are often collectors themselves, could identify with. Professor Thorne, in attempting to level with her subjects, repelled them:

> . . . as I crouched, watching and scribbling, on the sidelines of a basketball game, a girl came up and asked, "What are you doing?" "A study of children and what they play." "Do you wanna be a teacher?" she asked. "I am one. I teach sociology, ever hear of that?" "No." "It's the study of people in groups." "Well, goodbye," she said, running off.[30]

Many observers have noticed that children tend to separate by sex on the playground, even when they mix freely in classes and at home, and that their games and styles of play differ. Iona Opie takes this for granted, as if it were natural law. She remarks that boys are "more egotistical, enterprising, competitive, aggressive, and daring."[31] Girls "enjoy talking as a purely social activity, and take far more interest in people."[32] They are hospitable, helpful, conciliatory, and "infinitely cosy."[33] On the other hand, she notes that boys "are quite often to be seen crying (whereas I cannot remember ever having seen a girl in tears in the playground)."[34]

Barrie Thorne also sees differences between the play of boys and girls. She finds that boys' groups tend to be larger, that they form "'gangs,' 'teams,' or groups of 'buddies,' while girls organize themselves into smaller, more intimate groups and friendship pairs."[35] She also points out with some irritation that boys have ten times the play area of girls, and yet insist on invading and interrupting girls' games.

Iona Opie remarks that "food and sex are two of the children's principal interests"[36] and that the most exciting moments on the playground are when boys chase girls or vice versa. Professor Thorne also observed this activity, and others which brought the sexes together in what she calls "border areas" to engage in the antagonistic or mock antagonistic contacts she calls "borderwork."[37] Her account of these activities is one of the most interesting things in *Gender Play*. It also cannot help but remind some readers of the relations between the sexes that they have observed in so-called "adult" life.

According to Barrie Thorne, borderwork is a form of "interaction across—yet based on and even strengthening—gender boundaries."[38] These actions, she says, "often teeter between play and aggression, and heterosexual meanings lurk within." They arouse "excitement, playful elation, anger, desire, shame, and fear."[39] In a pattern she often observed, a member of one sex insults a member of the other, who then chases him or her. Sometimes several boys may chase one or several girls, or vice versa. The children Barrie Thorne watched often actively provoked these chases; indeed, she mentions one group of girls who spent their time on the playground "in an open-ended search for ritual contact with boys,"[40] an activity that can also sometimes be observed at adult parties and professional meetings.

In some of these chasing games, known as "catch-and-kiss," the runner is kissed when caught. Such kisses, however, are more aggressive than affectionate, and may even be contaminating, as Barrie Thorne points out. The schools she visited had rigid pecking orders, and in each class there were one or more children whose rank was so low that contact with them was polluting; in the language of the playground, which some readers may recall, they had "cooties." Girls low in the pecking order were known as "cootie queens," and could infect anyone who touched them. Low-status boys might also have cooties, but were not called "cootie kings."

Both boys and girls could give cooties, but boys did not give cooties to other boys. Most significant, perhaps, all girls, no matter what their social rank, could contaminate boys; in the Michigan elementary school cooties was also known as "girl stain."[41] Barrie Thorne observes that even objects associated with girls, like valentines, could be contaminating. Though she does not mention this, the belief sometimes survives into adulthood. Men can be contaminated by wearing women's clothes, or reading "women's novels" or magazines. Not long ago many men were told by writers like Robert Bly that modern urban life as a whole is intrinsically feminine and therefore weakening.

At the schools Barrie Thorne studied, there were ritual cures for "cootie" contamination, the most interesting of which was a contraption made of folded paper called a "cootie catcher," with which one could pick off invisible cooties from the infected person.[42] Adult men too can be decontaminated, according to Bly—though with considerable expenditure of time and money—by going into the woods away from women, chanting, and beating drums.

The idea of the female as intrinsically polluting, of course, has a long history. In many cultures menstruating women are dangerous, and among gypsies women below the waist are *marimay* (taboo); a man can be polluted merely by stepping over their legs. Urban and suburban Americans are supposed to be free of such beliefs, but Barrie Thorne's book suggests that this is not the case. She also notes, as others have, that the girl who joins boys' games and is identified as a tomboy does not lose social status or become contaminated, whereas the boy who is seen playing jump rope is called a sissy and moves to the bottom of the pecking order. The same processes, of course, can be observed in adult life.

The flip side to this magical belief system, as Barrie Thorne remarks, is that persons who are identified as polluting have power because they can threaten to pollute: "If a girl is designated as having cooties or threatens to plant a dangerous kiss, it is the boy who has to run."[43] Of course it is not always gender that makes someone possibly contaminating. I recently heard students at Cornell discussing the problems involved in inviting "creepy" relatives to a wedding. Naturally, they did not use the word *pollution,* but they vividly pictured how unpleasant it would be to have Uncle X or Cousin Y sitting at the table or slobbily kissing the bride and groom, and said that "everything would be spoiled" if they were there.

In *The People in the Playground* Iona Opie does not mention observing a belief in the contaminating effect of some children on others. It is hard to know whether it did not exist, or whether it seemed so obvious that she did not report it. Given what we know about British society, the latter seems most likely; but it is also possible that in England children remain ignorant of such magical theories until they reach secondary school. It would be most interesting to know whether Barrie Thorne would find a system of infectious touch operating in Hampshire; and to discover what Iona Opie would make of an American playground.

POETRY BY AND FOR CHILDREN

THERE are two main sorts of children's poetry. The first, which we all still know and enjoy, unless we have wholly forgotten our own youth, is composed by children themselves and by grown-ups who recall what it was like to be a child. The second sort is written for children by adults who wish, often with the best intentions, to educate, inspire, or caution the young. A few of these poems are enjoyed, but most are remembered, if at all, because we were forced to read or even to memorize and recite them when we were in school.

Whatever the prevailing adult taste in poetry for children, girls and boys themselves have continued to choose and create hundreds of wonderful anonymous rhymes. These verses survive sometimes for hundreds of years, and are passed on from generation to generation. Often their authors are lost, and they can only be dated approximately by internal evidence or by the time of their first appearance in print. For example:

> I asked my mother for fifty cents
> To see the elephant jump the fence.
> He jumped so high
> He touched the sky,
> And he never came back till the Fourth of July.

Nobody knows for sure who wrote this, or when, but it would be a good guess that the lines were composed in America, because of the reference to our national holiday, and between 1880 and 1920, when there were still many small traveling circuses and an entrance fee of fifty cents would have been reasonable. It has one of the classic marks of the nursery rhyme: the matter-of-factly described but fantastic event.

The anonymous verses that are passed down from one child to another often seem trivial if not irrational, but some of them are full of meaning. They are more than just a kind of primitive art: they are also primitive magic. Children are ritualists; they believe in the power of certain gestures and words. Oaths and promises are binding; charms influence events; counting-out rhymes call upon the powers of fate. Even the simplest verse can have an almost magical effect. The child who is taunted with the rhyme "April fool's gone past / You're the biggest fool at last"[1] may—as I know from experience—feel contaminated with stupidity until she or he has shouted back the magical counterspell:

> Sticks and stones
> May break my bones,
> But words will never hurt me.[2]

The great achievement of Iona and Peter Opie, the famous British folklorists, was to recognize years ago the power and fascination of children's rhymes, games, and pastimes. When they were young and unknown, living in the depths of the country and so poor that they occasionally dined on nettle soup, they began to study the origin and meaning of children's folklore. Today their works, from *The Oxford Dictionary of Nursery Rhymes* on, are classics in the field.

The Opies' first collection, *I Saw Esau,* appeared in 1947. For a long time this book was out of print and unavailable; finally, ten years after Peter Opie's death, it was reissued with abundant colored illustrations by Maurice Sendak that are as entrancing— and sometimes as shocking—as the text. The contents of *I Saw Esau* are not the traditional songs of Mother Goose, but verses like the one quoted above, many heard firsthand from contemporary British children. Most of them, as Iona Opie puts it in her new introduction, "were clearly not rhymes that a grandmother might sing to the grandchild on her knee. They have more oomph and zoom; they pack a punch."[3]

Because this is a British collection, some of its contents may be unfamiliar to American readers. Among my favorite discoveries is a curse disguised as an apology:

> I beg your pardon,
> Grant your grace;
> I hope the cows
> Will spit in your face.[4]

I also liked the matter-of-fact correction to a well-known proverb:

> The rain it raineth all around
> Upon the just and unjust fella:
> But chiefly on the just because
> The unjust stole the just's umbrella.[5]

I Saw Esau also draws on the remarkable depth and breadth of information that Iona and Peter Opie brought to all their works. Its lighthearted notes reveal an impressive knowledge of

British history and literature, biblical legends, detective fiction, rural dialect, and music-hall songs—among other specialties. "Thomas a Didymus, hard of belief," who "Sold his wife for a pound of beef,"[6] for instance, turns out to be Doubting Thomas, the apostle who was not convinced Christ had risen from the dead. The notes also contain information on juvenile fortune-telling and the best way to make a bonfire.

Equally remarkable is the Opies' unfailing identification with the child's point of view. *I Saw Esau* includes several versions of the well-known rhymes that counter the "ridiculous, oft-repeated enquiry by people who no doubt know the answer perfectly well."[7] As an American version has it:

> "What's your name?"
> "Butter and tame.
> If you ask me again
> I'll tell you the same."

Many of the entries relate to school and lessons, usually taking an unfavorable view of them. Often they parody the Latin that children in Britain, for centuries, have been made to learn at an early age. When spoken aloud these serious, incomprehensible lines resolve into a Cockney chant:

> Brutus adsum jam forte,
> Caesar aderat.
> Brutus sic in omnibus,
> Caesar sic inat.[8]

Translation:

> Brutus 'ad some jam for tea,
> Caesar 'ad a rat.
> Brutus sick in omnibus,
> Caesar sick in 'at.[9]

As children understand instinctively, ritual language (like poetry) is different from ordinary language. Speaking the correct words in the correct order is essential, and when this is not done, the force of the rhyme or spell or taunt dissolves. To Americans some of the verses in *I Saw Esau,* though familiar, may sound painfully wrong. "That's not right!" they may cry, just as they would have done as children. "That's not the way it goes!" This primitive reaction, of course, only proves how important these apparently simple rhymes once were to us, and how much we owe to Iona and Peter Opie for preserving them.

A good sampling of the sort of "children's poetry" that is written by adults for the instruction of the young appears in *The Oxford Book of Children's Verse in America,* edited by the gifted American poet Donald Hall. His anthology provides a fascinating historical record of how both poetry and childhood have been viewed from *The Bay Psalm Book* to Shel Silverstein and Nancy Willard.

The poems thought suitable for boys and girls in the seventeenth and eighteenth centuries, as Hall points out in his fine introduction, "appear to twentieth-century eyes wholly impossible for children."[10] Their message is almost unrelievedly moral and gloomy. As *The New England Primer* puts it:

> In Adam's fall
> We sinned all.

> While Youth do cheer
> Death may be near.[11]

The doctrine of original sin as interpreted by the Puritans justified the damnation of infants who were not of the elect, even though they personally had committed no fault. Their fate was described by Michael Wigglesworth in what now sounds like the curse of a maddened parent whose baby will not stop howling:

> But get away without delay
>   Christ pities not your cry:
> Depart to Hell, there may you yell,
>   And roar eternally.[12]

Of course, as Donald Hall says, this was not the only message received by children of the period; they also must have heard the old nursery rhymes and songs, and their lessons were often taught by means of lighthearted mnemonic verses that can still be found in some collections of Mother Goose rhymes.

> Great A, little a, bouncing B,
> The Cat's in the cupboard and can't see me.

By the early nineteenth century the message of doom had given way to a more moderate piety leavened by sentiment. Gradually, the influence of the Romantic movement was taking over. The child was no longer a helpless, possibly damned soul or an imp of Satan, but a holy innocent—sometimes too holy for this world. Popular nineteenth-century poems were full of good little girls and boys carried off by the angels; a late but at the time tremendously popular example of the type is Eugene Field's "Little Boy Blue," which describes the loyalty of the dead child's abandoned toys:

> Aye, faithful to Little Boy Blue they stand,
>   Each in the same old place—
> Awaiting the touch of a little hand,
>   The smile of a little face.[13]

The same sort of sentimental impulse appears in some of the rhymes that have entered oral tradition, like "Mary Had a Little

Lamb" and "Three Little Kittens." It is no accident, I think, that both these poems are about animals: contemporary children's magazines and annuals were full of verses about birds and beasts, expressing sympathy for what were then called "Our Dumb Friends" and often pointing a gentle SPCA moral.

The mid– and late nineteenth century was the heyday of the storytelling poem, often used as a recitation piece in school or at family gatherings. If you were born more than fifty years ago, you may have read or even recited some of the best-known of these poems like Longfellow's "Paul Revere's Ride" and Whittier's "Barbara Frietchie"—patriotic themes were especially popular. The most famous of them, the classic "A Visit from St. Nicholas," long attributed to Clement Clarke Moore,[14] is often read aloud in schools today.

Toward the end of the nineteenth century, when America was becoming increasingly urban and industrial, there was a flood of nostalgic verses celebrating rural childhood and the rural past, sometimes in dialect. Those of James Whitcomb Riley, such as "Little Orphant Annie" and "The Raggedy Man," still appear in some modern collections of poetry for children.

In the early twentieth century there was a fashion in children's poetry for what now seems a particularly cloying sort of supernatural whimsy: fairies at the bottom of my garden and practically everywhere else. Most of this verse was British, and it is underrepresented in Donald Hall's anthology, though he includes Morris Bishop's brilliant counterattack, "How to Treat Elves":

> I met an elf man in the woods,
>   The wee-est little elf!
> Sitting under a mushroom tall—
>   'Twas taller than himself!
>
> "How do you do, little elf," I said,
>   "And what do you do all day?"

"I dance 'n fwolic about," said he,
   " 'N scuttle about and play, . . .

" 'N then I play with the baby chicks,
   I call them, chick chick chick!
'N what do you think of that?" said he.
   I said, "It makes me sick.

"It gives me sharp and shooting pains
   To listen to such drool."
I lifted up my foot, and squashed
   The God damn little fool.[15]

The anthologies and magazines of the 1920s and 1930s attempted to introduce children to modern poetry, particularly imagism and free verse, without great success, to judge by my own experience and that of my friends. Children don't have much interest in poems that lack rhyme, rhythm, action, and humor, though a few of these verses, such as Carl Sandburg's "The fog comes / on little cat feet" still appear in modern collections. What they like is drama, rhythm, and rhyme, and especially humor. When it came time to choose poems for classroom recitation, we passed up Sandburg and Pound and H. D. in favor of Vachel Lindsay and Laura E. Richards. I remember a tearful struggle over who would get to recite Richards's "Eletelephony," which begins:

Once there was an elephant
Who tried to use the telephant—
No! No! I mean an elephone
Who tried to use the telephone—[16]

In the 1930s social consciousness entered many collections of verse for children. They included poems such as Vachel Lindsay's "Factory Windows Are Always Broken," and for the first time contained a representative selection from black writers. Toward the end of the decade and through World War II there was a resurgence of patriotism. Nineteenth-century favorites were dusted off and reprinted, and selections from Stephen and Rosemary Benét's brilliant *A Book of Americans* found their way into many anthologies.

The collections of the 1950s and early 1960s, as might be expected, tended to be conservative; but the late sixties and the seventies brought a flood of radical and counterculture anthologies of children's poetry. Some of them discarded most of the work of the past in favor of brand-new, not always name-brand verse recommending free expression, hugging, sexual equality, and a mystical attitude toward nature. There is not much poetry of this type in Hall's anthology, but it is well represented by John Ciardi's "The Man Who Sang the Sillies," which celebrates a sixties sort of childlike euphoria, concluding:

> . . . That The Luckies are The Happies, and the
>   Happies are the Sillies
> And the Sillies are the sweetest that I know.[17]

It is perhaps too early to characterize the children's poetry of the eighties and nineties. The most striking change I have noticed in looking through recent collections is a shrinkage in the length of the poems. A hundred years ago a grade-school child was thought quite capable of reading a serious, even tragic thirty-five-stanza poem like Celia Thaxter's ballad about the slave trade, "The Cruise of the Mystery"; more recently poems by Ogden Nash that ran to fifteen or twenty stanzas were widely reprinted. Today, children's attention span is assumed to be incredibly short, and they are also thought not to have much interest in poems about heavyweight social issues. I wonder if we are not underestimating them—or, even worse, creating the kind of disinterest we assume.

In the introduction to his anthology, Donald Hall speculates on these matters, remarking that very likely "our contemporary fashions in children's verse, which favor humor and nonsense, will one day seem as quaint as pieties about dead children."[18] It is hard to think he may be right, but you never know.

LOUDER THAN WORDS:
CHILDREN'S BOOK ILLUSTRATIONS

O NCE upon a time, the only illustrations of nursery rhymes and fairy stories were the ones that appeared in the minds of their audience: children to whom their parents recited the old verses about Jack and Jill or the cow that jumped over the moon, and people of all ages who heard the classic tales told aloud, perhaps on winter evenings around a cottage fire, or on a summer night that was too warm and star-sprinkled for sleep.

Those days are over. Today, we don't need to visualize these tales and rhymes for ourselves; others have already done it for us—sometimes brilliantly and sometimes badly. As children, when we sat in a circle for story hour, or were read to at bedtime, we were shown the pictures that "went with" a fairy tale or a Mother Goose rhyme. Before we heard "Cinderella" we saw her picture on the cover of the book or Disney video. And since we were children, we assumed the portrait was accurate; we didn't realize that it was only one person's idea of what the heroine and her fairy godmother and the prince looked like.

It is natural, perhaps, to wish sometimes that we still lived in an oral culture, and could form our own pictures of the classic stories and rhymes. But illustrations can add something as well as take it away. The coming together of a gifted artist and a great children's classic is always interesting. If the union is successful, the work will be reinterpreted, given not only new life but also a new and different meaning. It may even be, essentially, re-born, rising like a new-fledged phoenix from the ashes of an earlier incarnation.

Each age, of course, gets a different species of phoenix. The style of children's book illustration is a changing guide, not so much to what children are like in any generation, but to how adults perceive them, or would like to perceive them.

Printed versions of fairy tales have been appearing for more than three hundred years, but the earliest ones had few or no pictures. When Perrault's tales first appeared in 1697, there was only one small, simple woodcut illustration for each story. Some of them were inaccurate; the woodcut that accompanied the first edition of "Red Riding-Hood," for instance, shows an undis-guised wolf leaping onto the bed of a woman who is far too old to be Red Riding-Hood and too young to be her grandmother.

Pictures like these are unlikely to have interfered much with mental images of the stories. The words were still what counted, as the frontispiece of the book makes clear: it shows an old woman in peasant costume sitting by a fireside, telling a story to three children. A sign on the wall behind her reads: *Contes de Ma Mère l'Oye* (literally, "Tales of My Mother the Goose"). It was under that title that the book appeared in early English editions, with the same kind of small, crude woodcuts. In 1861, however, there was a French edition of Perrault's tales in which the pic-tures dominated the stories, and presented alarming visions of their worst moments. For this deluxe volume Gustave Doré, who was already famous for his editions of Rabelais and Dante, created full-page black-and-white illustrations that seem likely to terrify any child. It is true that many classic fairy tales are intrinsically frightening, and not only those of Perrault. Hansel and Gretel are imprisoned by a cannibalistic witch, Snow-White's stepmother plots her death, and a whole series of giants try to kill Jack. But Doré underlines the horror. His "Puss in Boots" is larger than any real cat; he has sharp teeth and dangerous-looking claws, and wears a huge plumed hat and a necklace of mouse skulls. The swollen, pop-eyed ogre in "Hop-O-My-Thumb" leans threateningly over the head of the bed in which his five little daughters sleep; he holds a huge knife with which he will cut their throats. Even more disturbing in some ways is Doré's famous illustration for "Red Riding-Hood." It shows the wolf, wearing the murdered grandmother's ruffled cap, in bed with a wide-eyed, half-naked little girl who seems to have just realized that she is about to be eaten or raped or both. These are frightening stories, Doré is telling us: children, especially girls, are in great danger. Brilliant though these pictures are, it is no wonder that they are seldom reprinted in modern collections.

After Doré, most illustrations of the classic fairy tales provided a softer and less frightening vision. Though the best-known stories often contain violent events, artists tended to avoid depicting them. Instead they chose earlier moments in the plot, when danger is only hinted at. For "Red Riding-Hood," for instance, most nineteenth- and twentieth-century illustrators show the heroine meeting the wolf in the forest. If they picture her in her grandmother's cottage, she is fully dressed and standing at a safe distance from the wolf. She does not look frightened yet, but stares at him with a blank or puzzled expression.

Two of the most famous early-twentieth-century illustrators, Arthur Rackham and Edmund Dulac, followed this pattern in their illustrations to the classic fairy tales. They emphasized the beauty, charm, and mystery of the stories, avoiding any suggestion of violence. In Rackham's illustrations to "Hop-O-My-

Thumb," for instance, the ogre is asleep, and he looks skinny and foolish rather than threatening. In Edmund Dulac's version of the stories, everything is bathed in a romantic blue mist. Ogres do not appear, nor do Cinderella's cruel stepmother and stepsisters. Dulac's Bluebeard scowls at his disobedient wife, but he is un- armed, and she seems embarrassed rather than frightened.

"Bluebeard" is in many ways the most disturbing of Per- rault's best-known stories, because the murderous villain is not a wolf or an ogre but the heroine's own husband. In many late- nineteenth- and early-twentieth-century editions this story is set in the Near East, and the translation is sometimes altered to fit. In both Rackham collections, Bluebeard's castle is a Moorish palace, and his formerly anonymous wife is called "Fatima."

Of course, the farther the setting of a fairy story is from our own world, the less disturbing its dark side seems. Perhaps this is one reason why many illustrators not only choose a seventeenth- or eighteenth-century background for the fairy tales, but portray every castle and court as a kind of aristocratic dream-Versailles. Edmund Dulac's Good Fairy and Arthur Rackham's Cinderella both wear eighteenth-century ballgowns, and Cinderella has a tall powdered Marie Antoinette hairdo. Later artists, especially in America, have sometimes set the tales even farther in the past: Trina Schart Hyman, for instance, locates her alluring 1977 ver- sion of "Sleeping Beauty" in the early Renaissance.

Terrifying or enchanting, beautiful or grotesque, most illus- trations of the classic fairy tales in the nineteenth and early twentieth century had one thing in common: they pictured a three-dimensional world, full of realistically depicted people, trees, cottages, beds, shoes, pumpkins, and mice. When super- natural beings appeared, they too were portrayed in realistic detail. These pictures were complex and fascinating; it was possible to return again and again to them, finding new things each time.

But in the mid–twentieth century a new kind of fairy-tale illustration appeared, when comic books and the Walt Disney studios made these old stories even more famous as animated cartoons. In the process, however, they often turned their characters into two-dimensional caricatures. Disney also reintroduced or even emphasized the occasional cruelty and violence of the tales. Cinderella's stepmother, so seldom pictured by earlier artists, reappears in the Disney version, looking angry and cruel, and accompanied by sneering ugly sisters and a nasty tomcat. The evil fairy in "Sleeping Beauty" is a blue-skinned black-caped villainess who soon becomes a thirty-foot fire-breathing dragon.

The flat, simple colors and shapes of the Disney illustrations may have helped to moderate these frightening images. But the final effect was to trivialize the fairy tale. Cinderella and Sleeping Beauty and Snow-White become doll-like figures, apparently made of the same colored plastic as their clothes and furniture, and the settings look like painted backdrops. Perhaps to counteract this unreality, the period of the stories has often been moved forward. In the Disney version Cinderella and her relatives wear the fashions of the 1890s, and Sleeping Beauty has a 1950s hairdo and party dress. Disney also softened the tales by adding moments of contemporary cuteness: Snow-White is taken in by comic dwarves, Cinderella is befriended by cartoon mice and birds, and Sleeping Beauty's powerful fairy godmother becomes small and fat and ridiculous.

Where gifted artists like Doré and Dulac and Rackham made supernatural figures seem real, the Disney studios reduced even human beings to cartoons. The effect of this, of course, was increased by the fact that animated films, instead of illustrating one or two moments from each fairy tale, encouraging the reader to visualize all that went before or after, necessarily picture the whole story, leaving no space for the imagination. Popular as they are, such films have made it even harder—perhaps impossible—for children to find their own way into a magic world.

The first surviving collection of nursery rhymes was published in London in 1744, and in this and most later eighteenth-century and early-nineteenth-century collections they were illustrated only with small woodcuts—sometimes with whatever woodcuts happened to be on hand in the print shop, without much relevance to the verses. Usually these pictures showed contemporary landscapes and costumes. But in the mid–nineteenth century, as printing techniques improved, the illustrations began to grow in size and number, and eventually to overwhelm the brief texts. As with the folktales, there were three dominant styles: realistic, fantastic, and comic.

Most common, especially at first, were realistic illustrations, one classic example of which is what is now called the *Original Mother Goose* (1916) illustrated by Blanche Fisher Wright, still in print and widely available. Many similar editions have appeared since, and more continue to be published.

The pictures in these books are often attractive, though they sometimes give the impression of having been drawn from life by a not very original student artist. Jack and Jill are real children climbing a three-dimensional hill. The cow does not jump over the moon, she only appears to; artists explain away the fantasy by providing a low viewpoint and a moon low on the horizon, and a human figure who runs away with both the dish and the spoon. The implied message of such illustrations is that the rhymes take place in a world much like that of the child who is reading the book, and that the events in them might in fact occur. Collections of this type often seem to emphasize the pedagogical nature of some of the verses; they become warnings against theft:

Tom, Tom, the piper's son
Stole a pig and away he run.
The pig was eat and Tom was beat,
And he went crying up the street.

or against telling tales ("Tattle-tale Tit, thy tongue shall be slit"), or whining:

"Baa baa, black sheep, have you any wool?"
"Yes sir, yes sir, three bags full.
One for my master and one for my dame,
But none for the little boy that cries in the lane."

They recommend conventional good behavior:

Early to bed and early to rise
Makes a man healthy and wealthy and wise.[1]

As any parent knows, some of the classic rhymes, like folk-tales, may be frightening. Mice have their tails cut off, beggars are invading town, the ladybird's children are burned up, and Cock Robin is dead. Realistic artists found various ways to soften the dark side of these verses. One common strategy was to set the scene in the past.[2] The custom started early: almost everyone in the popular nineteenth-century nursery-rhyme books of Walter Crane and Randolph Caldecott wears eighteenth-century fashions. In Kate Greenaway's *Mother Goose,* which first appeared in 1881, the children inhabit a preindustrial village world and have high-waisted Regency clothes and hairstyles. Ever since then it has been common for realistic illustrations to picture nursery-rhyme characters as living in an earlier time: Tasha Tudor, for instance, sets her pictures in Colonial America.[3]

A very different approach is evident in the elaborate, fantas-

tic creations of artists like Arthur Rackham, who imagine the
events of the rhymes as taking place in a magical but contemporary world. In his *Mother Goose* (1913), "Hi diddle diddle, the
cat and the fiddle" is the occasion for a glimpse into a mysterious, surrealistic world. The old man in the wood is a goblin,
while Miss Muffet's spider is nearly as large as she is and has a
shiny top hat; but most of the children wear the clothes of Rackham's own time. In the Blanche Fisher Wright edition, Mother
Goose is a kindly old woman in Elizabethan costume; Rackham's Mother Goose is a witch in a peaked black hat, who rides
her goose as if it were a broomstick. Other nonrealistic artists
imagine the world of the rhymes as more benevolent: Jessie
Wilcox Smith's Mother Goose is a huge white bird, much larger
than life size, who shelters two small children under her out-
spread wings. In the Vollard edition of 1915, illustrated by Frederick Richardson, each verse is floated in a rectangular cloud
above an elaborate painting, providing a collection of brilliantly
colored landscapes into which an imaginative boy or girl can
walk. The implication of all these artists, and many like them
who followed, is that the world of the nursery rhymes is a surrealistic kingdom that contemporary children can enter.

A third type of illustration presents nursery rhymes as essentially humorous, often in a cartoon style. It stresses not the down-
to-earth simplicity or magical strangeness of the rhymes, but
their comedy and energy. Arnold Lobel's *Random House Book
of Mother Goose* (1986) is a brilliant example of this approach.
His colorful, amusing drawings almost burst from the page.
Sometimes several rhymes are combined into one full-page or
double-page bouncy panorama; four verses that mention Christmas, for instance, become the text for a Dickensian snow scene.

For Lobel, the world of Mother Goose is an almost continu-
ous round of noise and fun and feasting. It is also "round" in another sense: everyone and everything in most of these pictures
is plump and roly-poly—people, chickens, cakes, mice, and

hills. The occasionally dark side of the verses is often canceled out by the illustrations. Johnny, who was "so long at the fair," is seen returning, farther down the page, laden with gifts. The three blind mice are only pretending to be blind and obviously won't lose their tails.

Readers who know other editions of *Mother Goose* may be disappointed by Lobel's. The comic exaggerations and loose, sketchy technique of his drawings, in which pencil lines and brush marks are visible, can destroy the illusion, reminding us that these pictures were made by a human hand and are not magical visions.

In the extreme case the pictures are only cutout symbols of the things and people they pretend to illustrate: flat, two-dimensional, brightly colored shapes sliding on a screen. The implication is that the verses have nothing to do with either reality or imagination; they are more or less pleasant rhymed non-sense, and need not frighten or admonish any child.

A related method of distancing the rhymes is to represent their characters as cute animals rather than human beings. Today, this is almost the standard choice of artists. In *Beatrix Potter's Nursery Rhyme Book,* a 1984 compilation illustrated with vignettes from her earlier work, almost all the characters are rabbits, squirrels, and mice, including the old woman who lived in a shoe and Little Jack Horner. This tradition continues, and is sometimes combined with a cartoon style of drawing. In *My Very First Mother Goose* (1996), edited by Iona Opie and illustrated by Rosemary Wells, Mother Goose is a large white goose, and almost everyone else is a rabbit, though they wear contemporary children's clothes.

There are, of course, advantages in turning Jack and Jill and all their friends into rabbits and bears and dogs and cats. Theoretically, if the illustrations to an American children's book are to be truly representative, the artist must make sure that all social classes are shown; that half the characters are male and half female; and that out of every ten, six are pink, one black, one Hispanic, one Asian, and one Native American—a tedious project. The animals in children's book illustrations are neither white nor nonwhite, neither rich nor poor, and often, as far as one can tell, they are neither male nor female. Any child can identify with them.

Recently, a few gifted illustrators have deliberately updated the Mother Goose rhymes, often adding more recent verses. One striking early example is Willy Pogany's 1928 edition, which sometimes suggests the paintings of Lionel Feininger. Pogany's Mother Goose rides over skyscrapers and chimneys, and the pretty maid going a-milking is accosted by a dude in a new convertible with a New York State license plate.

Most remarkable of all are Maurice Sendak's brilliant and innovative illustrations, which without adding a single word sometimes expand a simple verse into a complex story. His wonderful drawings for a new edition of Iona and Peter Opie's *I Saw Esau* (1992)—there is one on almost every page—do far more than illustrate the text.[4] They provide answers to the riddles and make jokes (in one picture, for instance, a mother silently turns into a tree to shelter her child from the rain, and then turns back again). They may tell a story that is only implicit in the rhyme, or introduce new characters: a lion as well as a child is shown spying on Esau, and dogs and cats frequently comment on the action by means of speech-balloons. The most amazing events are matter-of-factly portrayed, sometimes in drawings that, like the rhymes they accompany, may give the adult reader a moment's pause, as with:

> I one my mother.
> I two my mother.
> I three my mother.
> I four my mother.

I five my mother.
I six my mother.
I seven my mother.
I ate my mother.[5]

In the accompanying series of sketches, the baby does literally eat its mother.

Especially interesting are the pictures that illustrate two or more verses simultaneously, suggesting that the world of nursery rhymes, illogical and strange as it may seem, is whole and interconnected. In one picture there is a complete family, created from three different rhymes: it includes Nelly Bligh, who caught a fly;[6] Sam, the dirty old man who "washed his face in a frying pan";[7] and their baby, Moses, who "supposes his toeses are roses."[8] The protagonists of a fourth rhyme are visible through the window of the family's house.

At other times, a character from one rhyme reappears in the illustration to another: the grinning baby "made of bread and gravy" on page 60 is seen again later as a brown pudding that is at the same time also a baby. There are many other echoes and connections, and any observant child will have a fine time tracing them. Adult readers may be equally amused by the frontispiece, which shows Iona and Peter Opie, Maurice Sendak, and Sebastian Walker (the publisher of this collection) as nocturnal birds with human heads roosting in a moonlit forest. Below them two children sleep, guarded by a dog. (It is noticeable that Peter Opie, who according to report was a somewhat prickly character, has the sharpest talons.)

Soon after this book appeared, Maurice Sendak would use his art to create complex stories from simple, even apparently nonsensical verses. In *We Are All in the Dumps with Jack and Guy* (1992) two old rhymes are the nominal framework for a tale in which "the moon's in a fit," wicked rats play cards, and two shabby men rescue a homeless brown-skinned boy from an orphanage. The result brilliantly and scarily evokes the dark side of contemporary city life.

The artist Wallace Tripp has also created three wonderful collections of rhymes and short poems that are just the jumping-off point for his imagination. His pictures suggest that childhood and the world are full of variety and fun. They are also full of jokes and portraits of famous historical and literary figures. In *Marguerite, Go Wash Your Feet* (1985), for instance, Albrecht Dürer, Gertrude Stein, Ulysses S. Grant, John Wayne, Robert, Amy, and James Russell Lowell, Charlie Chaplin, Bertrand Russell, Dracula, Robinson Crusoe, King Kong, and the casts of *The Wizard of Oz* and *The Wind in the Willows* can be seen—and there are probably many others I haven't yet identified. The comically charming rabbits and bears and foxes and lions for which Tripp is deservedly famous also appear. A child can enjoy the book without recognizing most of these figures, but they will add tremendously to the amusement of any grown-up who reads it aloud.

Adults today usually read books without pictures, and unless they have the misfortune to see the film version before they open a novel, they can still create images of its characters and settings in their own minds. For children it is very different. They recognize images long before they can read, and even if not every page is illustrated, those that are guide their imagination. What the artist chose to portray, and how, may deeply affect their view of the book—and perhaps of all books. They will see them as beautiful, mysterious, funny, frightening, or boring, according to their experience. If they are to find the world of literature wonderful rather than uninteresting or terrifying, we must give them the best possible editions of the classics of children's literature.

ENCHANTED FORESTS AND SECRET GARDENS: NATURE IN CHILDREN'S LITERATURE

WHEN I was seven years old, my family moved to the country, and my perception of the world entirely altered. I had been used to regular, ordered spaces: labeled city and suburban streets and apartment buildings and parks with flat rectangular lawns and beds of bright "Do Not Touch" flowers behind wire fencing. Suddenly I found myself in a landscape of thrilling disorder, variety, and surprise.

As the child of modern, enlightened parents I had been told that many of the most interesting characters in my favorite stories were not real: there were no witches or fairies or dragons or giants. It had been easy for me to believe this; clearly, there was no room for them in a New York City apartment building. But the house we moved to was deep in the country, surrounded by fields and woods, and there were cows in the meadow across the road. Well, I thought, if there were cows, which I'd seen before only in pictures, why shouldn't there be fairies and elves in the woods behind our house? Why shouldn't there be a troll stamping and fuming in the loud, mossy darkness under the bridge that crossed the brook? There might even be one or two small hissing and smoking dragons—the size of teakettles, as my favorite children's author, E. Nesbit, described them—in the impenetrable thicket of blackberry briars and skunk cabbage beyond our garden.

No longer a rationalist, I began to believe in what my story-books said. Suddenly I saw the landscape as full of mystery and possibility—as essentially alive. After all, this was not surprising: it was the way most people saw the natural world for thousands of years, and the way it was portrayed in the stories I loved best.

For me, and I think for most children who have really known it, untamed nature seemed both powerful and sentient—a conscious force. The simplest rhymes assumed this: "Rain, rain, go away! Come again some other day," my sister and I chanted as the gray drops blurred the glass. The clear implication was that the rain could hear us, even if it chose not to do as we asked. This didn't seem strange; after all, nature often spoke by signs— the rainbow that marked the end of the storm, the groundhog that did or did not see its shadow on February second. Beasts and birds and plants predicted the future, and they even knew what other people secretly thought of us, revealing this through the petals of a daisy: "He loves me, he loves me not, he loves me a little, he loves me a lot, he loves me not at all." Even the distant stars could, if they chose, grant our wishes: "Star light, star bright, first star I see tonight . . ."

In fairy tales it was clear that nature was magical. This magic was concentrated in the forest, often referred to as an enchanted forest. If you were a fairy-tale hero or heroine, that was where you went or were sent to find adventures, in contrast to the or-dinary world of the village. What you found in the forest might be wonderful or terrible or both. There were wolves there and bears and deer, some of whom might be princes or princesses in disguise; there were houses made of cake and candy, dragons and giants, witches and dwarves. If you met anyone or anything in the magical world of nature, it was important to be polite, kind, and helpful, since they had the power to assist, or thwart you, to change your life.

The underlying message of folklore and fairy tales was that nature is alive, aware of us—that it must be treated with care and respect. This was well illustrated in the Grimms' tale "Mother Holle." It begins with a girl whose mother does not love her, preferring her lazy sister. In a state of despair the heroine jumps into a well, but instead of drowning she finds herself in a strange meadow full of flowers. She doesn't just sit there and grieve; she gets up and starts walking, and presently, the story says, "she came to a tree that was full of apples and it cried to her: 'Oh, shake me! shake me! my apples are all ripe!' So she shook the tree till the apples . . . were all down, and when she had gathered them into a heap, she went on."[1]

You may have noticed that the heroine of this story does not eat the apples. Instead of using them to satisfy her own needs, she cooperates with nature, helping the overburdened tree and recognizing its needs. She walks on, and presently she comes to a little house where there lives an old woman called Mother Holle, who is a domestic version of the pagan German nature goddess Holde. We know who she really is because, like Holde, she is in charge of the weather; when she describes the job she is offering our heroine, she says, "Take care to make my bed well, and shake it . . . till the feathers fly, for then it will snow on earth."[2] The girl does as she is told, and when she goes home she is rewarded with gold. Her lazy, greedy sister jumps into the same well and finds herself in the same meadow, but she refuses to cooperate with nature. She will not help the apple tree or shake the feather bed properly, and she comes home covered with tar.

Fairy tales made it clear that nature could be both protective and destructive. If you were a princess who fell into an enchanted sleep, a hedge of flowers and thorns would grow up around your castle. It would shield you for a hundred years, and destroy all the wrong princes who tried to cut their way through and get at you. Then it would open to admit your true love.

The powerful, magical image of nature found in folktales also appears in many classic and modern works of children's literature. Even the simplest stories sometimes contain messages about the mysterious importance of the natural world. Consider Margaret Wise Brown's *Goodnight Moon,* one of the most popular picture books of the twentieth century. It is a series of rhymed good nights addressed to all the most familiar objects of childhood. There is food (a bowl of mush), toys (a red balloon and a doll's house), articles of clothing and grooming (mittens and socks, brush and comb), pets (two kittens), and an old lady knitting, who may be a grandmother or a baby-sitter.

In the illustrations to *Goodnight Moon,* both the old lady and the child are rabbits, something that may seem strange at first, but is in fact one of their most important qualities. Like the animals in the fables of Aesop, they make the story universal. If the child in *Goodnight Moon* were human, the artist would have to show it as male or female, and as belonging to some ethnic group. But because the rabbit's gender and race are concealed, any reader or listener can identify with it.

Another advantage of many animal heroes is that they are classless; but the big green room is clearly that of a contemporary middle-class Western child. It is spacious and comfortable, contains pictures and books, and two clocks—being on time is important in this world. There is also a mechanical connection to the outside: a telephone. In 1947, when the book was published, for a child to have his or her own telephone was a great luxury; if Margaret Wise Brown had been writing the book today, the appliance on the little rabbit's bedside table might have been a computer.

Still, of all the things to which the story bids good night, the moon is the most important. We know this because it is mentioned in the title—after all, the book is not called *Goodnight Kittens* or *Goodnight Mittens,* though those phrases appear in the text. The moon also appears twice: once as a crescent in the picture of a cow jumping over the moon, and once as a full moon, surrounded by stars, outside the bedroom window. As the scene darkens, the objects and figures inside the "great green room" begin to fade, while at the same time the moon and stars glow brighter and brighter. They represent both nighttime and the natural world outside the little rabbit's bedroom; they will be there while he or she sleeps, and may bring dreams. The last lines recognize this, and also the fact that as we close our eyes the visual world disappears before the auditory one does:

> Goodnight stars,
> Goodnight air,
> Goodnight noises everywhere.[3]

As we drift toward sleep, the last thing we are usually aware of is sounds: people speaking and moving about downstairs, the crunch of traffic passing, a plane overhead, a dog barking, the chirping of birds as they settle for the night. The tale bids them farewell, the room is dark, and what we are left with is the image of the moon and stars.

Stories written for children are unique in many ways. It is not only that the central characters tend to be children: the whole world view is often different. For one thing, these stories, like fairy tales, usually have a happy ending. The good are rewarded and the bad are punished—as Oscar Wilde famously said in *The Importance of Being Earnest,* that is what fiction means.

It has been suggested that in classic children's literature food replaces sex as the principal source of excitement and sensual pleasure. Certainly there is something to this: think of the Christmas dinner of turkey and plum pudding in *Little Women,* or the picnic on Johnson's island in *Tom Sawyer* when Tom and Huck and Joe Harper eat fried bacon and cornbread. It might even be said that when food in children's books is inedible or unavailable, it is the emotional equivalent of bad or denied sex in an adult novel. One of the reasons *Alice in Wonderland* is sometimes unpopular with young readers may be that all Alice ever has to eat is drugs disguised as food ("Drink Me" and "Eat Me" their labels command), and they have supernatural and unpleasant effects. She never actually gets any tea at the Mad Hatter's tea party; and when she attends the banquet at the end of *Through the Looking-Glass,* she cannot eat the leg of mutton because it has been formally introduced to her, and as the Red Queen says, "It isn't etiquette to cut anyone you've been introduced to."[4]

If food replaces sex in children's books, what replaces religion? In the eighteenth and early nineteenth centuries, of course, books for children were full of religion, specifically Protestant Christianity; but by 1850 this theme was beginning to fade. By the end of the century, religion had largely been replaced by the worship of nature. Many children's classics of the late nineteenth and early twentieth centuries present nature as divine, naturally good, and full of inspiration and healing properties. There is a pagan tone to some of these books: the Christian god is replaced by spirits of another order, sometimes associated with natural features of the landscape, or with water or wind.

John Ruskin's "The King of the Golden River," written for the little girl he later married, and published in 1851, is an ecological fable in fairy-tale form. Its hero, little Gluck, has two selfish older brothers who, like greedy capitalists, have no interest in the beautiful valley where they live except for the profits they can make from it.

> They killed everything that did not pay for its eating. They shot the blackbirds, because they pecked the fruit . . . they poisoned the crickets for eating the crumbs in the kitchen; and smothered the cicadas, which used to sing all summer in the lime trees.[5]

The South-West Wind, who appears as a little old man in a long black cloak, is disgusted by the behavior of Gluck's brothers. As a result he no longer blows the rain clouds toward their valley, and it becomes dry and barren, "a shifting heap of red sand."[6] But when little Gluck shares his last drops of water, the land is restored to fertility, and the wicked brothers become two black stones.

Water and wind, in both folktales and children's classics, often have magical powers. In Charles Kingsley's *The Water Babies* (1863) a dirty, ignorant little chimney sweep is redeemed by falling into a river, where he meets wise maternal beings who comfort and educate him. In George MacDonald's *At the Back of the North Wind* (1871) a spirit of the air rescues the hero, sickly little Diamond, from a London slum and carries him off on several wonderful nighttime journeys.

Here in America, in the nineteenth century, nature was seen as transcendentally wonderful rather than magical. The scene that greets Tom Sawyer when he awakes on Jackson's Island in Twain's beloved Mississippi reads almost like a passage from Thoreau:

It was the cool gray dawn, and there was a delicious sense of repose and peace in the deep pervading calm and silence of the woods. Not a leaf stirred; not a sound obtruded upon great Nature's meditation. Beaded dewdrops stood upon the leaves and grasses . . .

Now, far away in the woods a bird called; another answered; presently the hammering of a woodpecker was heard. Gradually the cool dim gray of the morning whitened, and as gradually sounds multiplied and life manifested itself.[7]

The British writer Kenneth Grahame, like Twain, was in love with a river, though in his case it was the Upper Thames. His most famous book for children, *The Wind in the Willows* (1908), is full of Grahame's own love and reverence for nature, and also his expert knowledge of it. Unlike some writers, both for adults and for children, Grahame knew what flowers bloom .where and in what order, as in this famous passage about the riverbank:

Purple loose-strife arrived early, shaking luxuriant tangled locks along the edge of the mirror. . . . Willow-herb, tender and wistful, like a pink sunset cloud, was not slow to follow. Comfrey, the purple hand-in-hand with the white, crept forth to take its place in the line; and at last one morning the diffident and delaying dog-rose stepped delicately on the stage, . . .[8]

In *The Wind in the Willows* the River Thames is almost a character in its own right. When the Mole, in the first chapter of the book, suddenly comes upon it, he is overwhelmed, and sees it as alive, like himself:

Never in his life had he seen a river before—this sleek, sinuous, full-bodied animal, chasing and chuckling, gripping things with a gurgle and leaving them with a laugh . . .[9]

His friend the Water Rat perceives it even more intimately:

> It's brother and sister to me, and aunts, and company, and
> food and drink and (naturally) washing. It's my world and I
> don't want any other. What it hasn't got is not worth having,
> and what it doesn't know is not worth knowing.[10]

The Mole and the Rat live in cozy burrows in a safe and beautiful rural landscape, but sometimes they venture into the Wild
Wood, Grahame's sometimes sinister version of the enchanted
forest. The Wild Wood is dangerous: to survive there, as Rat says:

> . . . there are a hundred things one has to know. . . . pass-
> words and signs, and sayings which have power and effect,
> and plants you carry in your pocket, and verses you repeat,
> and dodges and tricks you practice. . . .[11]

When the Mole first enters the Wild Wood, he finds it exciting,
but he soon begins to imagine supernatural terrors:

> Twigs crackled under his feet, logs tripped him . . . trees
> crouched nearer and nearer, and holes made ugly mouths at
> him on either side. . . .
>   It was over his shoulder, and indistinctly, that he first
> thought he saw a face: a little evil wedge-shaped face look-
> ing out at him from a hole. When he turned and confronted
> it, the thing had vanished.[12]

The Rat realizes that the Mole is missing, and goes to rescue
his friend, but soon they are both hopelessly lost, and it begins
to snow heavily. They are saved by stumbling upon the underground home of their friend Mr. Badger, who is large and strong
enough not to be afraid of the weasels and stoats and foxes that
live in the Wild Wood. But the place remains threatening. When
they leave, ". . . looking back, they saw the whole mass of the

Wild Wood, dense, menacing, compact, grimly set in vast white surroundings."[13]

The natural world, and the animals that live there, are for Grahame more enduring than the human civilization that sometimes seems to have triumphed over them. The Wild Wood and the Badger's underground house, it turns out, are built on the ruins of an earlier human city. But as the Badger says:

> People come—they stay for a while, they flourish, they build—and they go. It is their way. But we remain. There were badgers here, I've been told, long before that same city ever came to be. And now there are badgers here again. . . . And so it will ever be.[14]

In a famous later chapter of the book, which takes place at the most magical time of the year, midsummer's eve, the Mole and the Rat see a figure whom they recognize as a great god. Kenneth Grahame does not name him, but since he plays pipes and leaves hoof marks in the turf, it is clear that he is the classical nature god Pan, who was traditionally the protector of small animals. At the time, Pan was a popular figure in British literature: he appears in much poetry and fiction, and also is suggested in the name of J. M. Barrie's boy hero, Peter Pan, who refused to grow up and lived on a wild island.

A. A. Milne's Pooh books can be seen as a quieter, more domesticated version of *The Wind in the Willows,* one in which humor plays a larger part. Most of Milne's characters are toys rather than live wild animals, and the natural dangers that sometimes threaten them are comparatively minor and humorous. Even Tigger, so violent and unpredictable at first, turns out to be lovable. Yet in Milne the power of nature is not underrated: there are floods and fogs and torrential rains and snowstorms, and the big tree in which Owl has built his house is blown down in a storm.

One common characteristic of nature in classic children's literature—as in real life—is that it is essentially random and mysterious. The Pooh books celebrate this. Nature cannot be totally understood or numbered: no one will ever know how many trees there are in the enchanted place at the top of the Forest.

> Christopher Robin knew that it was enchanted because nobody had ever been able to count whether it was sixty-three or sixty-four, not even when he tied a piece of string round each tree after he had counted it. Being enchanted, its floor was not like the floor of the Forest, gorse and bracken and heather, but close-set grass, quiet and smooth and green. It was the only place in the Forest where you could sit down carelessly, without getting up again almost at once and looking for somewhere else.[15]

Nature in the Pooh books is also timeless. Christopher Robin will grow up and go away to school, but (as he promises Pooh) in another sense he will always be there in the enchanted place at the top of the Forest. Of course, the idea of a magical grove of trees at the top of a hill has a long history and many reverberations in British folklore and history. Such places were the site of prehistoric burial mounds, and even today these groves of trees can be seen all over the British countryside; often these are the locations that contemporary British pagans and druids and white witches choose for their ritual celebrations. They are sacred places, somehow outside of time.

Not all classic children's books, of course, present nature as wholly benevolent or even manageable. In the tales of J. R. R. Tolkien, for instance, some trees, like Treebeard, are wise and good; others are malevolent. I love willows, which here in Ithaca are the first to put out leaves in the spring and the last to lose them in the fall. But in English folk tradition, as Tolkien knew, the willow plays an ambiguous role, and his willows are dangerous. This is also true in J. D. Rowling's Harry Potter books, where the Whomping Willows delight in slapping and hitting anyone who gets too close to them.

There are also classic children's books in which nature becomes irrational and unstable. In *Alice in Wonderland* animals boss Alice about and make fun of her, and in *Through the Looking-Glass* she enters a secret garden in which flowers criticize her nastily, and she cannot get anywhere no matter how fast she runs.

When nature is not irrational, it can still be dangerous, as in Laura Ingalls Wilder's Little House series or Baum's Oz books, though in both cases the dangers do not end tragically. Laura Ingalls Wilder's family must face a series of natural disasters, including blizzards, droughts, prairie fires, and a spring flood that nearly drowns young Laura. An entire book, *The Long Winter,* tells the story of the record-breaking winter of 1880–81, when the town is snowed in and people are on the edge of starvation, living on brown bread and water for weeks. But the Wilder family faces these hardships together and overcomes them; in the end they are stronger and closer because of what they have gone through.

The cyclone that carries Dorothy away in the first of Baum's Oz series, and the typhoon and earthquake that she encounters in later sequels, all have happy outcomes for Dorothy, since in every case she ends up in the Land of Oz. While these natural disasters are terrifying, she always faces them sensibly and bravely, just as she does other natural and supernatural dangers. She not only survives her adventures, she enjoys them. Clearly, the message of both Wilder and Baum is that nature, though unpredictable and sometimes frightening, is essentially a positive force, and that even apparently life-threatening natural catastrophes can have wonderful consequences.

*

Consciously or unconsciously, many of the authors of classic children's books are pantheists. For them nature is divine, and full of power to inspire and heal. But while for some nature must be sought in the enchanted forest, for others the magical location is a garden. In their books, to go into a garden is often the equivalent of attending a Sunday service, and gardening itself may become a kind of religious act.

For Frances Hodgson Burnett, nature was intrinsically healing. She herself was a dedicated gardener, the author of a how-to book about her own garden on Long Island. In her famous children's story *The Secret Garden* (1911) two extremely neurotic, unattractive, and self-centered children are transformed by a combination of fresh air, do-it-yourself psychology, and, most of all, the discovery and restoration of a long-abandoned rose garden.

When we meet Mary Lennox in India, she is a sickly, disagreeable child whose selfish, beautiful mother never had any interest in her. No one has ever loved her and she loves no one. But even then, to amuse herself, she plays at gardening, sticking scarlet hibiscus flowers into the bare earth. Later, after both her parents are dead, she is sent home to England, and then to Misselthwaite Manor on the Yorkshire Moors, which she hates at first sight. Things begin to improve when she is sent outdoors to play:

> . . . the big breaths of rough fresh air blown over the heather filled her lungs with something which was good for her whole thin body and whipped some red color into her cheeks and brightened her dull eyes. . . .[16]

Eventually Mary discovers the secret garden of the title. For years, like Mary herself, it has been confined and neglected. Then, as winter turns to spring, she begins to restore it, to weed and water and prune and plant, and in the process is herself restored to happiness and health. Later she is assisted in her task by a local boy, Dickon, and by her cousin Colin, who has spent most of his ten years indoors. Colin's mother died when he was born, and he has been brought up to believe that he is a crippled invalid. Yet he too is transformed and restored to health in the garden.

Sometimes in children's books the power of nature is embodied in a character, and Dickon in *The Secret Garden* is one of the most famous of these characters. Though he is only twelve years old, rough and uneducated, he is a kind of rural Pan, who spends most of his time, winter and summer, out on the moor. He can charm birds and animals by playing on his pipe, and knows all about plants—his sister says he "can make a flower grow out of a brick walk. . . . he just whispers things out o' th' ground."[17] It is Dickon who teaches Mary and Colin how to bring the secret garden back to life, and he is the first to declare that nature has spiritual powers; he calls it Magic.

"Everything is made out of Magic," [Colin says] "leaves and trees, flowers and birds, badgers and foxes and squirrels and people. So it must be all around us."[18]

Toward the end of the book the three children participate in what might be called a kind of spiritual communion when they have a natural-food picnic of "roasted eggs and potatoes and richly frothed new milk and oat-cakes and buns and heather honey and clotted cream."[19]

Frances Hodgson Burnett once wrote, "There ought to be a tremendous lot of natural splendid happiness in the life of every human being,"[20] and at the end of *The Secret Garden* she provides all her characters with a splendid if somewhat supernatural happy ending. Through a dream-vision of his dead wife the restored garden summons Colin's father, who has been wandering all over Europe in a state of hopeless depression for ten years. He returns to Misselthwaite Manor, and finds that the son he had thought of as a whiny, helpless invalid is now strong and full of energy, and in the famous last scene of the book they are reunited. Planting and weeding and watering can not only change a wasteland into a garden—the moral is, it can change your life. For more than twenty years, when I taught children's literature at Cornell, *The Secret Garden* was my students' favorite book, and this was the scene that moved them most.

For Cornell's most famous literary alumni, E. B. White, nature was also magical. His best-known book, *Charlotte's Web,* celebrates life on a New England farm that was based on his own farm in North Brooklin, Maine. The story is a kind of modern pastoral; it takes place over the course of a year, and is founded on close practical experience and observation. It tells how a little girl named Fern and a spider named Charlotte together preserve the life of a pig called Wilbur. They do it with words, in something of the same way that E. B. White, in his book, preserves a year in the life of a small New England farm in mid-twentieth-century America. The book has a happy ending for Wilbur, but it is also a kind of natural tragedy, since Charlotte, being a spider, has to die at the end of the summer. On a farm, White tells us, life and death are cyclical; but death always gives way to life, just as winter gives way to spring in this famous passage at the end of the book:

> "I heard the frogs today," said the old sheep one evening. "Listen! You can hear them now."
>
> Wilbur stood still and cocked his ears. From the pond, in shrill chorus, came the voices of hundreds of little frogs.

"Springtime," said the old sheep, thoughtfully. "Another spring." As she walked away, Wilbur saw a new lamb following her. It was only a few hours old.

The snows melted and ran away. The streams and ditches bubbled and chattered with rushing water. A sparrow with a streaky breast arrived and sang. The light strengthened, the mornings came sooner. Almost every morning there was another new lamb in the sheepfold. The goose was sitting on nine eggs. The sky seemed wider and a warm wind blew. The last remaining strands of Charlotte's old web floated away and vanished.[21]

When children read books like these, they are beginning to learn, or somehow already know, what their authors are trying to tell us: that nature is magical and that it can also be life-changing.

❧ NOTES

FOREWORD

1. Lurie, *Don't Tell the Grown-Ups.*
2. Applegate, *The Predator,* p. 14.
3. Ibid., p. 84.

THE UNDERDUCKLING: HANS CHRISTIAN ANDERSEN

1. Hans Christian Andersen, *The Fairy Tale of My Life,* quoted in Wullschlager, *Hans Christian Andersen,* p. 20.
2. William Bloch, quoted in Wullschlager, *Hans Christian Andersen,* p. 7.
3. Wullschlager, *Hans Christian Andersen,* p. 4.
4. Ibid., p. 135.
5. Andersen, *Fairy Tales and Legends,* p. 355.
6. Ibid., p. 205.
7. *H. C. Andersen's Levnedsbog,* edited by H. Topsoe-Jensen, quoted in Wullschlager, *Hans Christian Andersen,* p. 29.
8. In eighteenth-century France, however, there had been a vogue among aristocratic women for elaborate fairy tales of the sort associated with Charles Perrault and Madame d'Aulnoy, the author of "Beauty and the Beast."

9. Andersen, *Fairy Tales and Legends,* p. 107.

10. Edvard Collin, quoted in Wullschlager, *Hans Christian Andersen,* p. 109.

11. Letter to Edvard Collin, quoted in Wullschlager, *Hans Christian Andersen,* p. 110.

12. Andersen, *Fairy Tales and Legends,* p. 69.

13. Ibid., pp. 273–74.

14. Wullschlager, *Hans Christian Andersen,* pp. 70–71.

15. Journal for May 4, 1841, quoted in Wullschlager, *Hans Christian Andersen,* p. 200.

16. Wullschlager, *Hans Christian Andersen,* p. 6.

17. Ibid., p. 34.

18. Ibid., p. 215.

19. Ibid., pp. 49–50.

20. Ibid., p. 179.

21. Ibid., p. 5.

22. Andersen, *Fairy Tales and Legends,* p. 116.

23. Ibid., p. 226.

LITTLE WOMEN AND BIG GIRLS: LOUISA MAY ALCOTT

1. Alcott, *Little Women,* p. 179.

2. See Brumberg, "Something Happens to Girls," p. 30.

3. Alcott, *Little Women,* p. 227.

4. Ibid., p. 228.

5. Ibid., p. 390.

6. Ibid., p. 267.

7. Ibid., p. 446.

8. Elbert, *A Hunger for Home,* p. 210.

9. It is not true, as often asserted, that every girl identifies with Jo. Though many do, an informal survey of several hundred students at Cornell over the past thirty years has turned up many who related most closely to Meg, Beth, or Amy.

10. Alcott, *Little Women,* p. 164.

11. Ibid., p. 13.

12. Jo, however, is not allowed to continue writing the sort of popular and sensational adult stories, full of sex and violence, that her creator published. Under the influence of her future husband, Professor Bhaer, she feels "horribly ashamed" of them and throws them all into the fire.

13. Alcott, *Jo's Boys,* p. 50.

14. Elbert, *A Hunger for Home,* p. 242.

15. Hollander, "Portraying 'Little Women' Through the Ages," p. 11.

16. Alcott, *Little Women,* p. 14.

17. Ibid., p. 184.

THE ODDNESS OF OZ

1. See especially Carl S. Vogel's very interesting and perceptive analysis of Oz as a feminist, antiromantic world in "The Amazonia of Oz," *The Baum Bugle.*

2. Hearn, *The Annotated Wizard of Oz,* p. 12.

3. Carpenter, *L. Frank Baum,* p. 25.

4. Gardner and Nye, *The Wizard of Oz and Who He Was,* p. 47.

5. Carpenter, *L. Frank Baum,* p. 4.

6. Gage, *Women, Church, and State,* p. 13.

7. Matilda Gage Web site, p. 5.

8. Baum, *The Tin Woodman of Oz,* p. 156.

9. Baum, *Glinda of Oz,* pp. 21–22.

10. Baum, *Ozma of Oz,* pp. 96–98.

11. Baum, *Dorothy and the Wizard in Oz,* p. 26.

12. Ibid., p. 141.

13. Baum, *The Patchwork Girl of Oz,* p. 340.

14. Beckwith, "The Oddness of Oz," p. 87.

15. Ibid., p. 82.

16. Baum, *The Tin Woodman of Oz,* p. 31.

17. Ibid., p. 277.

18. Ibid., p. 278.

19. Ibid.

20. Baum, *The Wonderful Wizard of Oz,* p. 7.

21. Ibid., p. 12.

22. Wagner, *She Who Holds the Sky,* p. 7.

23. Baum, *The Marvelous Land of Oz,* p. 85.

24. Ibid., p. 89.

25. Ibid., p. 170.

26. Ibid.

27. Ibid., pp. 282–83.

28. Baum, *The Lost Princess of Oz,* p. 266.

29. Baum, *The Patchwork Girl of Oz,* p. 137.
30. According to some critics, the Oz books have always especially appealed to gay men and boys, who identify with the Scarecrow and the Tin Woodman, whom they see as homosexual friends; with Tip, the boy who becomes Ozma; or with the Cowardly Lion as played by Bert Lahr in the MGM film in a somewhat camp manner. At the Oz centennial in Bloomington, Indiana, the scholar Dee Michel, who is writing a book about the subject, gave an enthusiastically received talk on the topic.
31. Chaston, "If I Ever Go Looking for My Heart's Desire," p. 212.
32. Baum, *Glinda of Oz,* p. 13.
33. See Carpenter, *L. Frank Baum,* p. 134.

IS ANYBODY THERE? WALTER DE LA MARE'S SOLITARY CHILD

1. De la Mare, *Memoirs of a Midget,* p. 16.
2. Letter to Henry Newbolt, 18 February 1905, quoted in Whistler, *Imagination of the Heart,* p. 26.
3. Whistler, *Imagination of the Heart,* p. 25.
4. De la Mare, "Rupert Brooke and the Intellectual Imagination," 1919, reprinted in *Pleasures and Speculations,* p. 179.
5. De la Mare, *Pleasures and Speculations,* p. 176.
6. De la Mare, *The Listeners and Other Poems,* pp. 69–70.
7. De la Mare, "Maria-Fly," in *The Magic Jacket,* p. 75.
8. Bremser, "The Voice of Solitude: The Children's Verse of Walter de la Mare," p. 66.
9. Whistler, *Imagination of the Heart,* p. x.
10. Ibid.
11. Ibid.
12. Ibid., p. 122.
13. Ibid., p. 67.
14. Ibid., p. 36.
15. Quoted in Whistler, *Imagination of the Heart,* p. 199.
16. Whistler, *Imagination of the Heart,* p. 183.
17. De la Mare, *Memoirs of a Midget,* p. 267.
18. Ibid., p. 209.
19. Ibid., p. 33.
20. De la Mare, "The Wharf," *The Connoisseur,* pp. 283–306.
21. Whistler, *Imagination of the Heart,* p. 338.

22. Ibid., p. 299.

23. De la Mare, *Peacock Pie,* p. 8.

24. Ibid., p. 12.

25. Whistler, *Imagination of the Heart,* p. 338.

26. De la Mare, "Willows," in *On the Edge,* pp. 79–80.

27. Ibid., pp. 69–70.

JOHN MASEFIELD'S BOXES OF DELIGHT

1. Masefield, *Collected Poems,* p. 27.

2. A former student of mine who has become a professional astrologer believes that the split between Masefield's public and private selves was due to his having been born exactly at midnight. If you are born at midnight, he claims, your outer self is the exact opposite of your inner self, while if you are born at noon, they are identical. In this context, it is interesting that Masefield's most haunting children's book is called *The Midnight Folk.*

3. Hoffman, *Sewanee Review,* pp. 402–3.

4. Ibid., p. 394.

5. Ibid., p. 395.

6. Ibid., p. 394.

7. Ibid., p. 403.

8. Spark, *John Masefield,* p. 45.

9. Lamont, *Remembering John Masefield,* p. 9.

10. Ibid., p. 14.

11. Masefield, *So Long to Learn,* p. 10.

12. Ibid., p. 9.

13. Ibid., p. 10.

14. Babington-Smith, *John Masefield,* p. 17.

15. Masefield, *So Long to Learn,* p. 17.

16. Masefield, *New Chum,* pp. 170–76.

17. Babington-Smith, *John Masefield,* p. 32.

18. Ibid., p. 40.

19. Quoted in Sternlicht, *John Masefield,* p. 101.

20. Masefield, *Martin Hyde,* p. 1.

21. Ibid., pp. 75.

22. Ibid., pp. 66.

23. Ibid., pp. 66–67.

24. Ibid., pp. 165.
25. Ibid., pp. 222–23.
26. Ibid., pp. 299–300.
27. Masefield, *Jim Davis,* p. 175.
28. Ibid., p. 5.
29. Masefield, *The Midnight Folk,* p. 140.
30. Ibid., p. 38.
31. Ibid., p. 45.
32. Lamont, *Remembering John Masefield,* pp. 11–12.
33. Masefield, *The Box of Delights,* p. 83.

MOOMINTROLL AND HIS FRIENDS

1. W. Glyn Jones, *Tove Jansson.*
2. Jansson, *Moominsummer Madness,* p. 28.
3. Jansson, *Moominland Midwinter,* p. 52.
4. Jansson, *The Exploits of Moominpappa,* p. 43.
5. Jansson, *Moominpappa at Sea,* p. 186.
6. Ibid., p. 7.
7. Ibid., p. 100.
8. Ibid., pp. 13–14.
9. Ibid., p. 25.
10. Jansson, *Tales from Moominvalley,* p. 123.
11. Ibid., p. 141.
12. Jansson, *Moominvalley in November,* p. 29.
13. Ibid.
14. Jansson, *Tales from Moominvalley,* pp. 46–47.
15. Jansson, *Comet in Moominland,* pp. 29–30.
16. Ibid., p. 180.
17. Jansson, *Finn Family Moomintroll,* p. 131.
18. Ibid., p. 135.
19. Jansson, *Moominpappa at Sea,* p. 137.
20. Ibid.
21. Jansson, *Tales from Moominvalley,* p. 14.
22. Ibid., p. 16.
23. Jansson, *Moominvalley in November,* p. 75.

DR. SEUSS COMES BACK

1. Theodor Seuss Geisel, quoted in Morgan, *Dr. Seuss and Mr. Geisel,* p. 81.
2. The number of rejections for *And to Think That I Saw It on Mulberry Street* varies from one account to another; Seuss himself once said that he could never remember whether it was twenty-seven or twenty-nine.
3. Seuss, *The Cat in the Hat,* p. 61.
4. Nel, "Dada Knows Best," pp. 150–54.
5. Cott, *Pipers at the Gates of Dawn,* p. 28.
6. Philip Nel, however, suggests that Mayzie's flower may be a visual metaphor for the imagination, and if so, the point of the story is that her original ideas are exploited by a moneygrubbing agent ("Dada Knows Best," p. 180).

HAROUN AND THE SEA OF STORIES

1. Fenton, "Keeping Up with Salman Rushdie," p. 33.
2. Ibid.
3. Rushdie, *Haroun and the Sea of Stories,* p. 18.
4. Ibid., p. 26.
5. Ibid., p. 15.
6. Ibid., p. 79.
7. Ibid., p. 153.
8. Ibid., p. 102.
9. Ibid., p. 161.
10. Rushdie, in *The Wizard of Oz, BFI Film Classics.*
11. As Iff the Water Genie points out, the Hoopoe is a figure from ancient Near Eastern tales, where he "is the bird that leads all other birds through many dangerous places to their ultimate goal" (Rushdie, *Haroun and the Sea of Stories,* p. 64).
12. Rushdie, *Haroun and the Sea of Stories,* p. 107.
13. At one point, in an echo of *Through the Looking-Glass,* Haroun finds himself "standing in a landscape that looked exactly like a giant chess-board" (Rushdie, *Haroun and the Sea of Stories,* p. 73).
14. Rushdie, *Haroun and the Sea of Stories,* p. 185.
15. Ibid., p. 35.
16. Ibid., p. 37.
17. Ibid., p. 73.
18. Ibid., p. 129.

19. Ibid., pp. 192–93.
20. Ibid., pp. 82–83. The reference, apparently, is to the best-selling but rather simplistic children's stories by Sarah Ferguson, the Duchess of York, which feature a flying helicopter called Budgie.
21. Rushdie, *Haroun and the Sea of Stories,* p. 155.
22. Wolf, "Haroun and the Sea of Stories," p. 43.

THE PERILS OF HARRY POTTER

1. *Time,* p. 72.
2. Rowling, *Harry Potter and the Sorcerer's Stone,* p. 56.
3. Ibid., p. 66.
4. Ibid., p. 118.
5. The most striking exception to this rule occurs in C. S. Lewis's Narnia series, in which the wicked, power-mad figure is female.
6. Interview in *Time,* p. 73.
7. *Slate,* 24 August 1999.
8. *New York Times Book Review,* p. 39.
9. *Slate,* 25 August 1999.
10. Zipes, "The Phenomenon of Harry Potter," pp. 170–89.
11. Arms, *Pokemon and Harry Potter,* p. 74.
12. Abanes, *Harry Potter and the Bible,* p. 6.
13. Ibid., p. 137.
14. Ibid., p. 260.
15. Ibid., p. 66.
16. Ibid., p. 130.
17. Ibid.
18. Carvajal, "Marketing 'Narnia,'" p. 3.
19. Abanes, *Harry Potter and the Bible,* p. 241.
20. Lewis, *The Last Battle,* p. 154.
21. The British title of the book is *Harry Potter and the Philosopher's Stone;* the American edition substituted "Sorcerer" for "Philosopher" on the questionable assumption that most American readers know nothing about the history of alchemy and think of philosophy as dull.

WHAT FAIRY TALES TELL US

1. MacDonald, *The Light Princess,* p. 69.
2. DeMorgan, "A Toy Princess," p. 153.

3. Carter, "The Courtship of Mr. Lyon," p. 49.

4. Irving, "Rip Van Winkle," p. 82.

5. Hawthorne, "Feathertop," p. 272.

6. Baum, "The Glass Dog," p. 41.

7. Sandburg, *Rootabaga Country*, p. 9.

8. Ibid., p. 37.

9. Yolen, "The River Maid," p. 131.

BOYS AND GIRLS COME OUT TO PLAY: CHILDREN'S GAMES

1. Opie, *The People in the Playground*, p. 15.

2. Ibid., p. vii.

3. Ibid., p. 25.

4. Ibid., p. 183.

5. Ibid., p. 57.

6. Ibid., p. 22.

7. Ibid., p. 175.

8. Ibid., p. 181.

9. Ibid., p. 15.

10. Ibid., p. 81.

11. Ibid., p. 126.

12. Ibid., p. 35.

13. Ibid., p. 84.

14. Ibid., p. 35.

15. Ibid., p. 181.

16. Ibid., p. 109.

17. Ibid., p. 54.

18. Ibid., p. 19.

19. Ibid., p. 105.

20. Ibid., p. 43.

21. Professor Thorne uses the verb *lurk* more than once, suggesting— perhaps unconsciously—that unpleasant linguistic and sociological truths tend to lie in wait for the researcher like muggers or predatory beasts.

22. Thorne, *Gender Play*, p. 4.

23. Ibid., p. 2.

24. Ibid.

25. Ibid., p. 97.

26. Ibid., p. 24.

27. Ibid., p. 99.

28. Ibid., p. 27.

29. Opie, *People in the Playground*, p. 1.

30. Thorne, *Gender Play*, p. 18.

31. Opie, *People in the Playground*, p. 7.

32. Ibid., p. 8.

33. Ibid., p. 108.

34. Ibid., p. 7.

35. Thorne, *Gender Play*, p. 92.

36. Opie, *People in the Playground*, p. 9.

37. The fact that she chooses this term rather than "borderplay" may be an indication of how serious and perhaps exhausting she considers the interactions of children.

38. Thorne, *Gender Play*, p. 64.

39. Ibid., p. 66.

40. Ibid., p. 72.

41. Ibid., p. 74.

42. The same magical device is also widely used by children in fortune-telling, after answers to possible questions have been written on its various surfaces.

43. Thorne, *Gender Play*, p. 83.

POETRY BY AND FOR CHILDREN

1. Opie, *I Saw Esau*, p. 118.

2. Ibid., p. 35.

3. Ibid., p. 11.

4. Ibid., p. 62

5. Ibid., p. 58.

6. Ibid., p. 26.

7. Ibid., p. 146.

8. Ibid., p. 95.

9. Ibid., p. 153.

10. Hall, *The Oxford Book of Children's Verse*, p. xxiv.

11. Ibid., pp. 7–8.

12. Ibid., p. 6.

13. Ibid., p. 163.

14. According to recent research, however, the poem was in fact probably written by Henry Livingston, Jr. See Kirkpatrick, "Whose Jolly Old Elf Is That, Anyway?"

15. Hall, *The Oxford Book of Children's Verse,* pp. 232–33.
16. Ibid., p. 165.
17. Ibid., p. 262.
18. Ibid., p. xxiii.

LOUDER THAN WORDS: CHILDREN'S BOOK ILLUSTRATIONS

1. This particular rhyme, which has annoyed many children, inspired James Thurber's now-famous parody in *Fables for Our Time:*

> Early to rise and early to bed
> Makes a man healthy and wealthy and dead.

2. This is also true, of course, of illustrations to fairy tales, where it makes more sense: witches and dragons, giants and ogres, belong to the past.
3. Arthur Rackham, however, dresses most of his children in the fashions of his own time, the early twentieth century, though the adults seem to have bought their clothes a hundred years earlier. The effect is to suggest that contemporary children, the presumed readers of the verses, have somehow wandered into a much older world.
4. The collection was originally published in 1947, without Sendak's pictures.
5. Opie, *I Saw Esau,* p. 85.
6. Ibid., p. 47.
7. Ibid., p. 48.
8. Ibid., p. 45.

ENCHANTED FORESTS AND SECRET GARDENS:
NATURE IN CHILDREN'S LITERATURE

1. Grimm, "Mother Holle," p. 134.
2. Ibid.
3. Brown, *Goodnight Moon,* unpaged.
4. Carroll, *Through the Looking-Glass,* p. 262.
5. Ruskin, *King of the Golden River,* p. 11.
6. Ibid., p. 29.
7. Twain, *Tom Sawyer,* p. 121.
8. Grahame, *Wind in the Willows,* p. 50.
9. Ibid., p. 9.
10. Ibid., p. 15.

11. Ibid., p. 59.
12. Ibid., p. 53.
13. Ibid., p. 86.
14. Ibid., pp. 82–83.
15. Milne, *House at Pooh Corner,* pp. 170–72.
16. Burnett, *The Secret Garden,* p. 52.
17. Ibid., p. 99.
18. Ibid., p. 287.
19. Ibid., p. 310.
20. Thwaite, *Waiting for the Party,* pp. 75–76.
21. White, *Charlotte's Web,* p. 176.

♦ BIBLIOGRAPHY

Abanes, Richard. *Harry Potter and the Bible: The Menace Behind the Magick.* Camp Hill, PA: Horizon Books, Christian Publications, Inc., 2001.

Aiken, Joan. *A Bundle of Nerves.* London: Gollancz, 1976.

Alcott, Louisa May. *Jo's Boys.* Boston: Roberts Brothers, 1886.

———. *Little Men.* Boston: Roberts Brothers, 1871.

———. *Little Women.* Boston: Roberts Brothers, 1868.

Andersen, Hans Christian. *The Fairy Tale of My Life.* New York: Paddington Press, 1975.

———. *Fairy Tales and Legends.* London: The Bodley Head, 1978.

Applegate, Katherine A. *The Predator (Animorphs No. 5).* New York: Apple, 1996.

Arms, Phil. *Pokemon and Harry Potter: A Fatal Attraction.* Oklahoma City: Hearthstone Publishing, 2000.

Babington-Smith, Constance. *John Masefield: A Life.* New York: Macmillan, 1978.

Barthelme, Donald. *City Life*. New York: Farrar, Straus & Giroux, 1970.

Baum, L. Frank. *American Fairy Tales*. Chicago: George M. Hill, 1901.

———. *The Annotated Wizard of Oz*. Edited by Michale Patrick Hearn. New York: C. N. Potter, 1973.

———. *Dorothy and the Wizard in Oz*. Chicago: Reilly & Lee, 1908.

———. *The Emerald City of Oz*. Chicago: Reilly & Lee, 1910.

———. *Glinda of Oz*. Chicago: Reilly & Lee, 1920.

———. *The Lost Princess of Oz*. Chicago: Reilly & Lee, 1917.

———. *The Marvelous Land of Oz*. Chicago: Reilly & Lee, 1904.

———. *The Magic of Oz*. Chicago: Reilly & Lee, 1919.

———. *Ozma of Oz*. Chicago: Reilly & Lee, 1907.

———. *The Patchwork Girl of Oz*. Chicago: Reilly & Lee, 1913.

———. *Rinkitink in Oz*. Chicago: Reilly & Lee, 1916.

———. *The Road to Oz*. Chicago: Reilly & Lee, 1909.

———. *The Scarecrow of Oz*. Chicago: Reilly & Lee, 1915.

———. *Tik-Tok of Oz*. Chicago: Reilly & Lee, 1914.

———. *The Tin Woodman of Oz*. Chicago: Reilly & Lee, 1918.

———. *The Wonderful Wizard of Oz*. Chicago: Reilly & Lee, 1900.

Beckwith, Osmond. "The Oddness of Oz," *Children's Literature,* vol. 5 (1976).

Bremser, Martha. "The Voice of Solitude: The Children's Verse of Walter de la Mare," *Children's Literature,* vol. 21 (1993), p. 66.

Brown, Margaret Wise. *Goodnight Moon*. New York: Harper, 1947.

Browne, Frances. *Granny's Wonderful Chair*. London: Griffith and Farrar, 1857.

Brumberg, Joan Jacobs. "Something Happens to Girls," *Journal of the History of Sexuality,* vol. 4, no. 1 (1993), p. 30.

Burnett, Frances Hodgson. *The Secret Garden*. London: J. M. Dent & Sons, 1975.

Carpenter, Angelica. *L. Frank Baum, Royal Historian of Oz*. Minneapolis: Lerner Publications, 1992.

Carroll, Lewis. *The Complete Works of Lewis Carroll*. New York: Viking, 1989.

Carter, Angela. *The Bloody Chamber*. New York: Viking Penguin, 1979.

Carvajal, Doree. "Marketing 'Narnia' Without a Christian Lion," *The New York Times,* 3 June 2001, p. 3.

Chaston, Joel. "If I Ever Go Looking for My Heart's Desire," *The Lion and the Unicorn,* vol. 18 (1984), p. 212.

Clifford, Lucy Lane. *Anyhow Stories*. London: Macmillan, 1882.

Collier, John. *Presenting Moonshine*. New York: Viking, 1941.

Cott, Jonathan. *Pipers at the Gates of Dawn*. New York: Random House, 1983.

De la Mare, Walter. *Broomsticks and Other Tales*. London: Constable, 1925.

————. *The Connoisseur*. London: W. Collins, 1926.

————. *The Listeners and Other Poems*. London: Constable and Company, 1912.

————. *The Magic Jacket*. New York: Knopf, 1962.

————. *Memoirs of a Midget*. London: W. Collins, 1921.

————. *On the Edge*. London: Faber and Faber, 1930.

————. *Peacock Pie*. New York: Henry Holt and Company, 1924.

————. *Pleasures and Speculations*. London: Faber and Faber, 1940.

De Morgan, Mary. *On a Pincushion and Other Tales*. London: Seely, Jackson & Halliday, 1877.

Desy, Jeanne. *Stories for Free Children*. New York: McGraw-Hill, 1982.

Dick, Philip K. *The Collected Stories of Philip K. Dick*. Los Angeles: Underwood-Miller, 1987.

Dickens, Charles. "The Magic Fishbone," in *Holiday Romance*. Boston: Ticknor & Fields, 1868.

Disney's Cinderella. New York: Mouseworks, The Walt Disney Company, 1994.

Disney's Sleeping Beauty. New York: Mouseworks, The Walt Disney Company, 1994.

Doré, Gustav (illustrator). *Contes du Temps Passé,* by Charles Perrault. Paris: Hetzel, 1862.

Dulac, Edmund (illustrator). *Sleeping Beauty and Other Fairy Tales from the Old French, retold by Sir Arthur Quiller-Couch.* London: Hodder & Stoughton, 1910.

Dunsany, Lord. *A Dreamer's Tales*. New York: Boni & Liveright, 1919.

Elbert, Sarah. *A Hunger for Home*. New Brunswick: Rutgers University Press, 1987.

Erdrich, Louise. "Old Man Potchikoo," *Granta,* vol. 32 (Summer 1989).

Ewing, Juliana Horatia. *Old-Fashioned Fairy Tales*. London: Society for Promoting Christian Knowledge, 1882.

Fenton, James. "Keeping Up with Salman Rushdie," *The New York Review of Books,* 28 March 1991.

Gage, Matilda. *Women, Church, and State*. Chicago: C. M. Kerr, 1893.

Gardner, Martin, and Nye, Russel B. *The Wizard of Oz and Who He Was*. East Lansing, Mich.: Michigan State University Press, 1957.

Grahame, Kenneth. "The Reluctant Dragon," in *Dream Days*. London: John Lane, 1898.

———. *The Wind in the Willows*. New York: Scribner's, 1991.

Gram, Paul. "Wild About Harry," *Time,* 20 September 1999, pp. 72–73.

Greenaway, Kate (illustrator). *Mother Goose, or the Old Nursery Rhymes*. London: Frederick Warne & Company, 1881.

Grimm, Jacob and Wilhelm. *The Complete Grimm's Fairy Tales.* New York: Pantheon Books, 1944.

Hall, Donald, ed. *The Oxford Book of Children's Verse in America.* New York: Oxford University Press, 1985.

Hawthorne, Nathaniel. "Feathertop," in *Mosses from an Old Manse.* Boston: Ticknor & Fields, 1854.

Hoffman, Daniel. "Rubbish About Sending a Man to the Moon," *Sewanee Review,* vol. 101 (Summer 1993), pp. 394–403.

Hollander, Anne. "Portraying 'Little Women' Through the Ages," *The New York Times,* 15 January 1995, p. 11.

Irving, Washington. "Rip Van Winkle," in *The Sketch Book.* New York: C. S. Van Winkle, 1819–20.

Iyer, Pico. "The Playing Fields of Hogwarts," *The New York Times Book Review,* 10 October 1999, p. 39.

Jansson, Tove. *Comet in Moominland.* New York: Farrar, Straus & Giroux, 1990.

———. *The Exploits of Moominpappa.* London: Puffin Books, 1969.

———. *Finn Family Moomintroll.* New York: Farrar, Straus & Giroux, 1990.

———. *Moominland Midwinter.* New York: Farrar, Straus & Giroux, 1992.

———. *Moominpappa at Sea.* New York: Farrar, Straus & Giroux, 1993.

———. *Moominsummer Madness.* New York: Farrar, Straus & Giroux, 1992.

———. *Moominvalley in November.* London: Puffin Books, 1974.

———. *The Sculptor's Daughter.* London: Ernest Benn Ltd., 1968.

———. *Tales from Moominvalley.* New York: Farrar, Straus & Giroux, 1995.

Jones, W. Glyn. *Tove Jansson.* Boston: Twayne, 1984.

Kennedy, Richard. *Collected Stories.* New York: Harper & Row, 1987.

Kirkpatrick, David. "Whose Jolly Old Elf Is That, Anyway?" *The New York Times,* 26 October 2000, p. 20.

Lamont, Corlis. *Remembering John Masefield.* With an Introduction by Judith Masefield. Rutherford, N.J.: Fairleigh Dickinson University Press, 1971.

Lewis, C. S. *The Last Battle.* New York: Harper & Row, 1956.

Lobel, Arnold (illustrator). *The Random House Book of Mother Goose.* New York: Random House, 1986.

Lurie, Alison. *Don't Tell the Grown-ups: Subversive Children's Literature.* Boston: Little Brown, 1990.

MacDonald, George. *The Light Princess.* New York: Farrar, Straus & Giroux, 1963.

Malamud, Bernard. "The Jewbird," in *Idiots First.* New York: Farrar, Straus & Giroux, 1963.

Masefield, John. *A Book of Discoveries.* London: Wells Gardner, Darton & Co., 1910.

———. *The Box of Delights: When the Wolves Were Running.* London: W. Heinemann, 1935.

———. *Collected Poems.* London: W. Heinemann, 1923.

———. *Jim Davis.* London: Wells Gardner, Darton & Co., 1911.

———. *King Cole.* London: W. Heinemann, 1923.

———. *Martin Hyde: The Duke's Messenger.* London: Wells Gardner, Darton & Co., 1910.

———. *The Midnight Folk.* London: W. Heinemann, 1927.

———. *New Chum.* London: W. Heinemann, 1946.

———. *So Long to Learn.* New York: Macmillan, 1952.

Milne, A. A. *The House at Pooh Corner.* London: Methuen, 1928.

Mitchison, Naomi. "In the Family," in *Five Men and a Swan.* London: Allen & Unwin, 1957.

Morgan, Judith, and Morgan, Neil. *Dr. Seuss and Mr. Geisel.* New York: Random House, 1995.

Nel, Philip. "Dada Knows Best: Growing Up 'Surreal' with Dr. Seuss," *Children's Literature,* vol. 27 (1999), pp. 150–74.

Nesbit, E. *The Book of Dragons*. London: T. Fisher Unwin, 1900.

Opie, Iona. *The People in the Playground*. New York and London: Oxford University Press, 1993.

Opie, Iona, and Peter. *I Saw Esau: The Schoolchild's Pocket Book*. Illustrated by Maurice Sendak. Cambridge, Mass.: Candlewick Press, 1992.

Perrault, Charles. *Histoires, ou contes du temps passé*. Paris: Claude Barbin, 1697.

Pogany, Willy (illustrator). *Mother Goose*. New York: T. Nelson and Sons, 1928.

Potter, Beatrix (illustrator). *Beatrix Potter's Nursery Rhyme Book*. London: T. Warne, 1984.

Pyle, Howard. *Pepper and Salt*. New York: Harper and Brothers, 1885.

Rackham, Arthur (illustrator). *The Arthur Rackham Fairy Book*. London: Harrap, 1933.

———. *Mother Goose*. London: Heinemann, 1913.

Richards, Laura B. "The Golden Windows," in *The Golden Windows: A Book of Fables for Young and Old*. Boston: Little Brown, c. 1904.

Richardson, Frederick (illustrator). *Mother Goose: The Vollard Edition*. Chicago and New York: P. F. Vollard, 1915.

Rowling, J. K. *Harry Potter and the Chamber of Secrets*. New York: Arthur A. Levine Books, 1999.

———. *Harry Potter and the Goblet of Fire*. New York: Arthur A. Levine Books, 2000.

———. *Harry Potter and the Prisoner of Azkaban*. New York: Arthur A. Levine Books, 1999.

———. *Harry Potter and the Sorcerer's Stone*. New York: Arthur A. Levine Books, 1998.

Rushdie, Salman. *Haroun and the Sea of Stories*. New York: Granta Books, 1990.

———. Contribution to *BFI Film Classics: The Wizard of Oz*. London: British Film Institute, 1992.

Ruskin, John. *The King of the Golden River*. London: Smith Elder, 1851.

Sandburg, Carl. *Rootabaga Stories*. New York: Harcourt, Brace, 1922.

Sendak, Maurice. *We Are All in the Dumps with Jack and Guy*. New York: HarperCollins, 1992.

Seuss, Dr. (Theodor Seuss Geisel). *And to Think That I Saw It on Mulberry Street*. New York: Vanguard, 1937.

————. *Bartholomew and the Oobleck*. New York: Random House, 1947.

————. *The Butter Battle Book*. New York: Random House, 1984.

————. *The Cat in the Hat*. New York: Random House, 1957.

————. *The Cat in the Hat Comes Back*. New York: Random House, 1958.

————. *Green Eggs and Ham*. New York: Random House, 1960.

————. *Horton Hatches the Egg*. New York: Random House, 1940.

————. *Horton Hears a Who*. New York: Random House, 1954.

————. *I Can Lick 30 Tigers Today!* New York: Random House, 1969.

————. *If I Ran the Circus*. New York: Random House, 1956.

————. *If I Ran the Zoo*. New York: Random House, 1950.

————. *The Lorax*. New York: Random House, 1971.

————. *McElligot's Pool*. New York: Random House, 1947.

————. *Oh, the Places You'll Go!* New York: Random House, 1990.

————. *On Beyond Zebra!* New York: Random House, 1955.

————. *One Fish Two Fish Red Fish Blue Fish*. New York: Random House, 1960.

————. *Thidwick, the Big-hearted Moose*. New York: Random House, 1949.

————. *Yertle the Turtle and Other Stories*. New York: Random House, 1958.

————. *You're Only Old Once!* New York: Random House, 1986.

Sinclair, Catherine. *Holiday House*. Edinburgh: I. W. Whyte & Co., 1839.

Singer, I. B. *When Shlemiel Went to Warsaw & Other Stories*. New York: Charles Scribner's Sons, 1887.

Slate Magazine Web site (www.slate.com). "Will There Be Trouble with Harry?" 24 August 1999.

————. "Harry in the New World." 25 August 1999.

Spark, Muriel. *John Masefield*. London: Peter Nevill, 1953; London: Hutchinson, 1992 (revised edition).

Sternlicht, Sanford. *John Masefield*. Boston: Twayne, 1977.

Stockton, Frank. *The Bee-Man of Orn and Other Fanciful Tales*. New York: Charles Scribner's Sons, 1887.

Thorne, Barrie. *Gender Play*. New Brunswick, N. J.: Rutgers University Press, 1993.

Thurber, James. *Fables for Our Time*. New York: Harper & Row, 1951.

Thwaite, Ann. *Waiting for the Party*. New York: Scribner's, 1974.

Tommy Thumb's Pretty Song Book. London: Mary Cooper, 1744.

Tripp, Wallace. *Marguerite, Go Wash Your Feet*. Boston: Little Brown, 1985.

Twain, Mark. *The Adventures of Tom Sawyer*. Hartford, Conn.: The American Publishing Company, 1876.

Vogel, Carl S. "The Amazonia of Oz," *The Baum Bugle*, vol. 26, no. 2 (Autumn 1982), pp. 4–8.

Wagner, Sally Rosch. *Matilda Joslyn Gage: She Who Holds the Sky*. Aberdeen, S. D.: Sky Carrier Press, 1998.

Warner, Sylvia Townsend. *The Cat's Cradle Book*. London: Chatto & Windus, 1940.

Wells, H. G. *Twelve Stories and a Dream*. London: Macmillan, 1903.

Whistler, Theresa. *Imagination of the Heart: The Life of Walter de la Mare*. London: Duckworth, 1993.

White, E. B. *Charlotte's Web*. New York: Harper, 1952.

White, T. H. *The Maharaja and Other Stories*. London: Macdonald, 1935.

Wilde, Oscar. *The Happy Prince*. London: D. Nutt, 1888.

Wilder, Laura Ingalls. *Little House in the Big Woods*. New York: Harper, 1932.

————. *Little House on the Prairie*. New York: Harper, 1935.

————. *The Long Winter*. New York: Harper, 1940.

————. *On the Banks of Plum Creek*. New York: Harper, 1937.

Wolf, Matt. "Haroun and the Sea of Stories," *Variety*, 16 November 1998–18 November 1998, p. 43.

Wright, Blanche Fisher (illustrator). *The Real Mother Goose*. Chicago: Rand McNally & Company, 1916.

Wullschlager, Jackie. *Hans Christian Andersen: The Life of a Storyteller*. New York: Simon and Schuster, 2001.

Yolen, Jane. *Neptune Rising*. New York: Philomel, 1982.

Zipes, Jack. "The Phenomenon of Harry Potter," in *Sticks and Stones*. New York: Routledge, 2000.

❧ INDEX

Note: Fictional characters appear with the title of the literary work in parentheses after the name.